Students Can't Pay Attention and Other Lies I Believed

This powerful book from mindfulness consultant Jenny Mills helps teachers overcome daily stressors and burnout by focusing on foundational skills – for both yourself and your students. Designed with busy educators in mind, the book doesn't add another item on people's plates – rather, the strategies act *as* the plate – affording you the capacity to better hold all of the things you are managing.

The book is centered around eight lies or myths about students and teaching, dismantled with a truth, followed by an easy-to-implement foundational skills lesson for teachers and students.

Mills shows how you can build attention control, executive functioning, and social-emotional learning in both yourself and your students, to help students thrive in school and in the real world, and to help you feel fulfilled in your teaching career.

Throughout, there are personal anecdotes, pause and reflect features, easy-to-implement teacher lessons to weave into the day, and student micro-lessons with modifications. As you refine the foundational skills, you'll be able to step into your power and feel more grounded and happier in your daily work in the classroom.

Jenny Mills, M.Ed., IMTA-P, is on a mission to change the world using mindfulness-based practices. You can find her at www.rootsandwingsonline.org or on LinkedIn: linkedin.com/in/millsjenny.

T0373581

Also Available from Routledge Eye On Education
www.routledge.com/k-12

Teaching Resilience and Mental Health Across the Curriculum:
A Guide for High School and College Teachers
Linda Yaron Weston

Mindfulness for Students:
A Curriculum for Grades 3-8
Wendy Fuchs

Everyday Self-Care for Educators:
Tools and Strategies for Well-Being
Carla Tantillo Philibert, Christopher Soto, Lara Veon

First Aid for Teacher Burnout, 2nd Edition:
How You Can Find Peace and Success
Jenny Rankin

Students Can't Pay Attention and Other Lies I Believed

16 Lessons to Improve Foundational Skills and Reclaim Your Classroom

Jenny Mills

Routledge
Taylor & Francis Group

NEW YORK AND LONDON

Designed cover image: © Getty Images

First published 2023
by Routledge
605 Third Avenue, New York, NY 10158

and by Routledge
4 Park Square, Milton Park, Abingdon, Oxon, OX14 4RN

Routledge is an imprint of the Taylor & Francis Group, an informa business

© 2023 Jenny Mills

Library of Congress Cataloging-in-Publication Data
Names: Mills, Jenny (Educational consultant), author.
Title: Students can't pay attention and other lies I believed : 16 lessons
to improve foundational skills and reclaim your classroom / Jenny Mills.
Description: New York, NY : Routledge, 2023. | Series: Routledge eye on
education | Includes bibliographical references. |
Identifiers: LCCN 2022053915 | ISBN 9781032326955 (hardback) |
ISBN 9781032157665 (paperback) | ISBN 9781003316275 (ebook)
Subjects: LCSH: Effective teaching. | Reflective teaching. | Teachers–Job stress.
Classification: LCC LB1025.3 .M555 2023 | DDC 371.102–dc23/eng/20230216
LC record available at https://lccn.loc.gov/2022053915

ISBN: 978-1-032-32695-5 (hbk)
ISBN: 978-1-032-15766-5 (pbk)
ISBN: 978-1-003-31627-5 (ebk)

DOI: 10.4324/9781003316275

Typeset in Palatino
by Deanta Global Publishing Services, Chennai, India

Access the Support Material: www.routledge.com/9781032157665

Support Material

Some of the resources in this book are also available on our website as free downloads, so you can easily print and use them. They are indicated with the Support Material icon .

To access the downloads, go to our website at www.routledge.com /9781032157665 and click on the link that says Support Material.

To all of the teachers who love to teach yet are struggling with all the other *stuff* that goes along with it - this is for you.

Contents

Acknowledgments

I would like to thank a few special people who provided tremendous support throughout this process. First, my husband Burton for believing in me, and providing the space and time required to complete this project. Thank you to my editors, Lauren Davis, Bill & Joyce Roca and Lucia Guardascione for your guidance and attention to detail. Special thanks to Dianne Kuhn and Brunna Dutkevitcz for the unwavering support of our family. I am incredibly grateful to all of the teachers whose stories, quotes, and experiences informed these pages, namely Megan and Renee Roca, Cari Jurgenson, and Maggie Sweeny.

Meet the Author

Jenny Mills, M.Ed., IMTA-P, is on a mission to change the world using mindfulness-based practices. An entrepreneur, author, international speaker and educator, Jenny believes that in order to create a sustainable teaching profession, we must develop the foundational skills of teachers and students. While serving as a special educator in NJ and Pennsylvania, Jenny realized that students and teachers lacked foundational skills like attention management, self-regulation, and emotional awareness. Without these skills, teaching and learning suffered.

Jenny developed her expertise as a meditation and mindfulness teacher at the University of Pennsylvania, and went on to open her business, Roots & Wings, LLC – a professional development organization that brings research-based interventions to K–12 schools and organizations. Jenny is currently a doctoral candidate at the University of Virginia and an adjunct faculty member at the University of Pennsylvania, Graduate School of Education. She is the Social-Emotional Learning and Trauma Coordinator at the Penn Literacy Network, creating and implementing coursework for teachers around the world.

When she isn't busy helping teachers, she is playing Legos and Barbies with her two young children, Talula and Zachary. In her spare time, Jenny enjoys listening to podcasts, running outside, and traveling.

You can find her at www.rootsandwingsonline.org or on LinkedIn: linkedin.com/in/millsjenny/.

1

Laying the Foundation for Sustainable Teaching and Learning

Introduction

The State of K–12 Educators

"How about instead of another professional development workshop on self-care, you give us more time to co-plan, less meetings, and fully fund our classrooms," scoffed a fifth-grade teacher, Jaime*, during a team meeting. Comments like this keep me up at night, because I know the thinking behind the comment. Like many educators today, in Jaime's mind being told to "be more resilient" and "take better care of herself" is just another way of blaming *her* for the dysfunction in her school. Sadly, nothing could be further from the truth.

I have spent my entire career serving in education. Sixteen years as a teacher, teacher educator, and consultant – and never have I seen the level of despair, burnout, and sheer exhaustion that I am observing now. According to the 2021 State of the U.S. Teacher Survey,

> nearly one in four teachers said that they were likely to leave their jobs by the end of the 2020–2021 school year, compared with one in six teachers who were likely to leave, on average, prior to the pandemic. Black or African American teachers were particularly likely to plan to leave.
>
> (Steiner & Woo, 2021)

---

* Names have been changed throughout the book.

DOI: 10.4324/9781003316275-1

High levels of teacher stress is not a new phenomenon. A widely cited study reports teacher stress levels similar to that of physicians and nurses (Greenberg et al., 2016). If teacher stress and burnout was an issue threatening the quality of our public schools prior to 2020, it is now a national crisis.

How Did We Get Here?

Over the last decade, teaching in American public schools has become unsustainable, as educators navigate school shootings, a global pandemic, racial injustice, climate change debates, political unrest, and an increasingly diverse student body. Teachers in underprivileged districts often manage additional stressors like overcrowding, unsanitary working conditions, and crumbling infrastructures.

"We thought this year would be better, since we were back to in-person learning. It's actually the hardest year yet," commented a 12th-grade teacher regarding the 2021–2022 school year. Just as public school teachers believed they had turned the corner on the COVID-19 pandemic, they faced new challenges: Culture wars. Banned books. Sex education. Learning loss. Lack of substitutes. Prayer in schools. Many public school teachers have made it clear that they are fed up with their working conditions by exiting the profession in droves. In 2021, nearly 1 million people quit jobs in public education, a 40 percent increase over the previous year (Packer, 2022). Those who remain are likely surviving, rather than thriving. In New Mexico, the National Guard was called upon to fill teaching vacancies as schools scrambled with COVID-19–related absences and resignations. I recently read a viral story on Twitter about a well-loved male teacher who quit teaching to work at Walmart instead, sharing how much happier, healthier, and better cared for he felt. There is much discussion of the "teacher shortage crisis," when ironically – there is no shortage at all.

> **Teachers didn't disappear – they made a statement.**

According to the first annual Merrimack College Teacher Survey, "44% reported likely to leave the profession in the next 2 years, 44% reported 'treated like professionals' by the public, and only 12% reported feeling very satisfied with their jobs" (Merrimack College Teacher Survey, 2022). Educators are no longer willing to sacrifice their mental, physical, and emotional health for a job that is grossly underpaid, overworked, and undervalued. I honestly cannot blame them.

As a country, we are long overdue for large-scale, multi-faceted systemic changes at all levels of education from our outdated teacher education programs to our overemphasis on standardized tests. This will take time, leadership, and persistence. But what can we do right now? How can educators harness their power as the most valuable resource in education and lead the way? Thinking critically about how we will enact transformative, systemic changes begins with our own self-reflection, which this book is designed to facilitate.

Creating a Foundation of Sustainability

Teachers are the most critical and influential factor in the success of future generations. We owe it to society to carefully consider how we develop, retain, and care for our educators. Hiring new staff to have over half of them leave the profession within five years is simply unsustainable from a business perspective. Researchers have estimated the cost of national teacher turnover at $8 billion per year (Sutcher et al., 2019). In essence, the American public continues to watch billions of tax dollars walk out of our schools year after year, while districts scramble to recruit, hire, and train new staff.

While better pay, more autonomy, and fewer initiatives would help teachers stay committed to the classroom, developing a set of critical skills to help navigate the stressors teachers face must come first and is desperately needed right *now*.

Attention, Executive Function, and Social-Emotional Learning

My training as an educator, coupled with my expertise in the field of mindfulness, has led to the development of a foundational skills model that links attentional control, executive functioning (EF), and social-emotional learning (SEL) skills. These three skill sets interact to form the foundation that teachers need to not just remain in the field, but lead the way in educational reform. In addition, students *also* need these foundational skills in order to learn and thrive in our classrooms and in the world.

Most K–12 teachers are expected to teach some sort of SEL curriculum, without ample training in developing these skills themselves. The foundational skills model contains the five broad interrelated areas of competence as defined by the Collaborative for Academic Social and Emotional Learning (CASEL).

It is possible that executive functioning skills and attentional skills are new terms for some teachers – these will be unpacked and defined in the chapters that follow.

Laying the Foundation for Sustainable Teaching and Learning

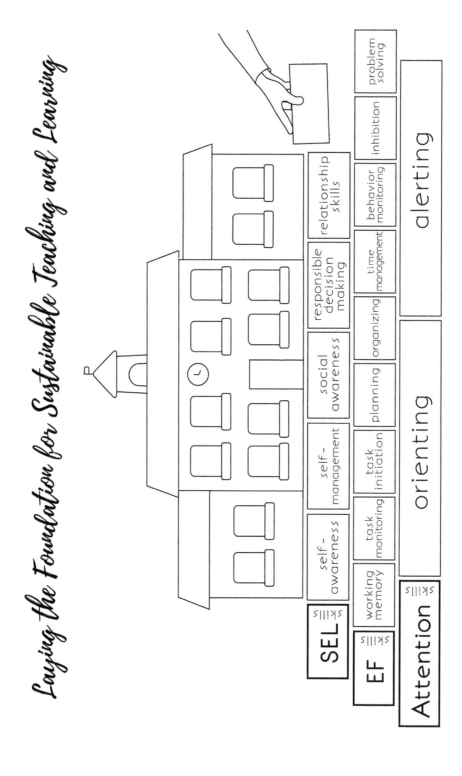

Structure and Use of the Text

Lies and Truths

Within these pages are the lies that I believed during my early years as a classroom teacher. These faulty beliefs were so buried in my subconscious that I didn't even realize they were there. In fact, it took many years of mindfully noticing my thinking to uncover them. It is only in hindsight that I see how these faulty beliefs colored my mood, my behavior, and my teaching career. Each lie is dismantled with a truth followed by an easy-to-implement foundational skills lesson for teachers and students.

I know that many teachers relate to these faulty beliefs, and some leave the classroom because of them. Frankly, I miss the classroom dearly, and regret not staying longer. Every September, I feel that first snap of fresh Fall air and miss greeting my students on the first day of school. I miss silly sock days, eating brownie bites with my colleagues during meetings, and listening to my students' stories about their weekend soccer tournaments. I miss the notes from students, the emails of gratitude from parents, and so much more. I wrote this book with the deep hope that the content of its pages may help teachers stay committed to their classroom, their students, and their love of teaching and learning.

Teachers Learning Alongside Students

Part of the pushback in implementing SEL, character education, or other *soft skill* curricula is that overextended teachers feel that they cannot handle *one more thing* – which is understandable. Rather than thinking about these foundational skills as *another content* or something added to teachers' plates, think of them as *the plate* – affording teachers the capacity to better hold all of the things they are managing. Rather than handing teachers yet another curriculum without proper training, this book encourages teachers to learn *with* students. Each chapter introduces a foundational skill for the teacher to learn and practice, followed by a student lesson targeting the same skill. Note that this is not a train the trainer model, and turnkey training is not recommended. Teachers cannot successfully teach students to hone foundational skills like managing attention, controlling impulses, and building self-awareness unless they are doing the work themselves.

Text Features: Anecdotes

Many real and uncensored personal anecdotes from my life as a teacher, teacher educator, and parent are included in this book, to help the text come alive and encourage teachers to make personal connections. One of my favorite teachers says that books are either windows or mirrors. I hope the anecdotes serve as mirrors, and show teachers that they are not alone in their struggles.

Text Features: Pause and Reflect

Learning is an interactive and iterative process between the individual and the text. Teachers learn best when they read, write, and reflect on not only the content of learning but the process. Ample space is provided for honest reflection in hopes it is put to good use.

> *Example*
>
> *Pause and Reflect*
>
> How can you relate to my experience co-teaching? What thoughts and emotions did you notice as you read the anecdote?
>
> _____
>
> _____
>
> _____

Teacher Lessons

Each chapter provides easy-to-implement practices to weave into a busy day. Do not skip these! The teacher lessons *mirror* the student lessons so that teachers can learn *with* their students. Teachers should spend at least a week working through each chapter to be sure there is enough time for the learning to solidify before moving on.

> **Example Student Microlesson**
>
> **Demonstrate: T**: "When someone throws an object to you, you have a reaction to catch it. It's not something you think about – it happens automatically. Some reactions are helpful – like catching objects or moving out of the way when someone walks too close in the hallway. Other reactions can get us into trouble, like talking back to a teacher, pushing someone on the playground, or sending a text message without thinking."
>
> **Participate: T**: "Let's try responding vs. reacting. Take out a book/something to read. I'm going to create some distracting noises around the room. You might stop and notice me, then choose to respond by taking a breath and focusing your flashlight of attention on your job – reading." The teacher spends 30 seconds stomping around the room, opening and closing doors, sharpening pencils, banging on a desk, etc. Students will giggle, which is okay! T: "Okay, stop reading. Turn and talk to a partner – what was it like to *choose a response*, notice me then continue to read, rather than become completely distracted and off task?" Emphasize that it is challenging.
>
> **Thread: T**: "Let's practice noticing the ways we react vs. respond to distractions during class. You also might notice how you can respond to challenging situations at home or at school."

Student Microlessons

A microlesson is a five to seven minute quick hit lesson that packs a powerful punch. The pace is brisk, the language is pointed and deliberate, and the learning is impactful. The microlessons may be used in any content area and across grades with little prep and no high-tech bells and whistles. Microlessons are structured around how the brain learns: First, teachers gain attention (hook) and then deliver instruction (demonstrate). Next, students participate in the learning. The most important step is how teachers thread and model the concept through their teaching. Without this step, the lesson hangs in the air without any direct application.

Note that teachers might choose to work through the text focusing only on the content and teacher lessons. Even without direct instruction, students benefit – academically and behaviorally – from teachers who are working on their *own* foundational skills.

Microlesson Differentiation and Modifications

The student microlessons have been used in small and large group learning environments, kindergarten through high school, in gym, art, speech, and chemistry. A variety of differentiation options are provided for upper and lower grades, English language learners, students with neurodiversity, gifted students, as well as considerations for students with a history of trauma. Students learn best when teachers provide differentiated entry points into the content being presented, therefore the microlessons are designed to accommodate the diverse needs of today's students. Note that the microlesson differentiation, modifications, and notes section are simply *suggestions* to help teachers think about these different populations. It is not feasible or realistic to differentiate every microlesson, but reading through the suggestions will help inform best practices in all content areas.

The Power of Connection

Teacher burnout has been exacerbated through our shift away from spaces to communicate, share in positive emotions, and authentically relate to our colleagues. The typical teacher works 54 hours per week, 25 hours of which are spent teaching students (Kurtz, 2022). As paperwork piles higher and common planning time dwindles (or disappears), teachers find themselves isolated and lacking genuine connection to their colleagues. Ideally, groups of teachers will work through this book together, either as a grade or subject-area team, or professional learning community. If teachers must work alone, informally sharing thoughts and reflections with other educators will prove beneficial.

The field of education is surely in crisis, and yet I know in my bones that we can change course. I believe in teachers. I know teachers are well trained, smart, and capable. I hope this book allows teachers to step into their power, hone their foundational skills, and do their job with a sense of confidence and groundedness.

References

Greenberg, M. T., Brown, J. L., & Abenavoli, R. M. (2016). *Teacher stress and health: Effects on teachers, students, and schools.* Retrieved from Pennsylvania State University, Edna Bennett Pierce Prevention Research Center: http://prevention.psu.edu/uploads/files/rwjf430428.pdf.

Kurtz, H. (2022, April 14). *A profession in crisis: Findings from a national teacher survey.* Edweek.org. www.edweek.org/research-center/reports/teaching-profession-in-crisis-national-teacher-survey?utm_source=eb&utm_medium=eml&utm_campaign=promo&utm_content=merri20220419&M=4354059&UUID=0974c0a6f86d794b01ea1c5e6ab832d7.

Merrimack College Teacher Survey. (2022). https://fs24.formsite.com/edweek/images/WP-Merrimack_College-Todays_Teachers_Are_Deeply_Disillusioned_Survey_Data_Confirms.pdf.

Packer, G. (2022, April). The grown-ups are losing it. *The Atlantic,* 11–14. www.theatlantic.com/magazine/archive/2022/04/pandemic-politics-public-schools/622824/.

Steiner, E. & Woo, A. (2021). *Job-related stress threatens the teacher supply: Key findings from the 2021 state of the U.S. teacher survey.* Research Report. RR-A1108–1.

Sutcher, L., Darling-Hammond, L., & Carver-Thomas, D. (2019). Understanding teacher shortages: An analysis of teacher supply and demand in the United States. *Education Policy Analysis Archives, 27*(35). http://dx.doi.org/10.14507/epaa.27.3696. This article is part of the special issue, *Understanding and Solving Teacher Shortages: Policy Strategies for a Strong Profession,* guest edited by Linda Darling-Hammond and Anne Podolsky.

2

The Lie

I Can Teach Kids to Read, but I Cannot Teach Kids to Focus

The Truth: Attention can and should be taught.

 Key Concepts in This Chapter:

★ Attention is the foundation of teaching and learning.
★ There are different types of attention.
★ Explicitly practicing managing attention is a game changing skill for teachers, students, and classrooms.

Sage on the Stage

When I was a classroom teacher, one of my fifth-graders, Luke*, was constantly staring off into space during math. After trying out all the usual tricks like moving his seat and providing frequent breaks, I finally asked Luke what he was thinking about. I will never forget this moment – he said he was thinking about whether he should wear sweatpants or shorts under his Halloween costume. In that moment I realized: I could control Luke's environment and redirect him until I was blue in the face, but I could not control where he placed his attention.

* All names have been changed.

DOI: 10.4324/9781003316275-2

During those early years as a classroom teacher, I could not shake the feeling that something was missing from my teacher education program and district-level training. How could I be expected to teach this ever-complex and vast amount of content when my students clearly could not pay attention, manage distractions, and independently engage with the learning process? "A lesson a day," I was told by my colleagues, "you have to keep up."

I tried helping Luke by doing what I thought was right: redirected, refocused, and when that didn't work – reprimanded. The problem with this approach was that it taught Luke nothing about how to manage *himself*. It offered him no insights into his own brain and how it worked. I was working hard as his manager while his role was passive. Someone once told me that I should not leave school more tired than my students, and I thought, "I am exhausted by the end of third period, let alone the end of the day." I was working harder than my students as their *sage on the stage* when what I really needed to do was be their *guide on the side*.

Pause and Reflect

Would you consider yourself the *sage on the stage*, doing most of the heavy lifting while your students passively receive information? When, if ever, do you become the *guide on the side*, allowing the students more autonomy and control?

_____

_____

_____

_____

_____

Pay Attention!

As a classroom teacher I had no idea how important it was to understand the mental faculty of attention. Not only did I not understand how to help my students manage their attention, I was also unaware of how my own (lack of) attentional control affected my teaching and my life. However, this did not stop me from telling my students to "pay attention" multiple times per day.

> **For many years I believed the lie that I could not teach my students *how* to pay attention – they had to do that on their own.**

Action and behaviors flow from beliefs, hence, believing this lie negatively impacted the decisions I made as an educator. If students could not be *taught* to pay attention or focus, then the following beliefs were also true:

♦ it was not my fault if distracted students missed important aspects of my lesson;
♦ disruptive behavior was inevitable; and
♦ attentional control is fixed; unchanging with age and experience.

Believing that I could not teach students to pay attention let me off the hook – one less thing to be responsible for teaching.

Like most teachers, I had no idea how to explicitly teach my students to manage their attention, their thinking, or their behaviors. Most of my students thrived while those that struggled to pay attention did just that – struggled. And so did I. I sat through many hours of professional development, yet no one could help answer this question: How do we get students to actually focus on the instruction I was delivering?

> **To create independent learners, teachers must shift from managing students to teaching them to manage themselves.**

Give Me Five

I was told by my grade-level team that attention could be "taught" by hanging a trusty and popular "Give Me Five" poster on the board. If you are a teacher, I guarantee you have seen this poster. But alas, even after I purchased and hung this trusty visual, my students still struggled to manage their attention and listen to instructions. A student could be looking right at me, but not be paying attention to what I was saying. Sound familiar?

Give Me 5

1. Eyes looking
2. Ears listening
3. Mouth quiet
4. Hands still
5. Brain thinking

Pause and Reflect

Check your background knowledge on this topic. What do you already know about teaching students to manage their thinking, attention, and learning? How do you teach students to pay attention, if at all?

_____

_____

_____

_____

_____

Pay Attention – or Suffer the Consequences

Attention is best conceptualized as a system of processes in the brain. Similar to a muscle, the more you work the system, the more nimble it becomes. Dr. Amishi Jha, a highly regarded neuroscientist and attention researcher at the University of Miami, says "attention is a currency," "a superpower," and is needed for "nearly every aspect of our lives" (Jha, 2021). Willingly or not, we all *pay* attention in this unspoken economy and allow marketing, media, and our electronic devices to rob us of our most important commodity.

In essence, a human life is made up of a series of moments strung together. The only moment we truly can experience is this moment right now. All of the moments before this moment are the past, and all of the moments right after this are the future. We forget the significance and urgency of being present for this moment now, where our life is actually happening. Instead, we get lost in thoughts of the past or future, or simply distracted by something else. We are literally missing the moments of our lives. All. The. Time.

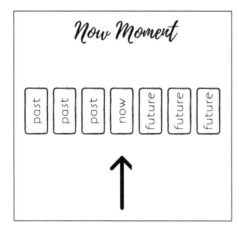

Sometimes, my moments are experienced like this:

I feel an ache in my neck. Deep sigh. Put a stack of papers down. Pick up my phone. Look at the screen. Press a button. Smile at a picture of my friend's child being silly. Scroll. Read an advertisement for new pants. Scroll. Take a sip of coffee. Look up. See my own child's face. Hear my child's request for snacks. Pretty relatable – am I right? I am in control of where I place my attention. Hence, learning to manage my attention dictates how and if I truly experience and inhabit the moments of my life, rather than live my life as an autopilot robot worrying about the future and rehashing the past.

> **Understanding and taking charge of attention can not only enhance productivity, but also improve mood, deepen relationships with others, and allow us to notice and connect with joy in everyday moments.**

Attention is the portal through which we experience our inner and outer worlds. Through this portal we hear our inner thoughts and desires, we see our baby's first steps, we imagine the characters in our favorite summer novel, and much more. It is amazing to realize that a mental faculty that we do not even notice is so very important to our happiness, wellbeing, and success in life.

Orienting System: The Flashlight

Let's refer back to the "Give Me Five" poster. The image of a smiling and seemingly attentive student, eyes looking and body still, leads me to believe that the poster is referencing what is referred to as **selective attention** or the **orienting system of attention**. We engage in this system when we hold our attention to an object or task for any length of time. Many mindfulness teachers and executive

Orienting System of Attention

alerts

hunger

thoughts

composing text

function coaches refer to selective attention as the flashlight in the brain. With the flashlight, we direct our attention to where we want it to go and hold it there (sustain) while filtering distractions. "Where you point it becomes brighter, highlighted, more salient," while the information outside the beam "stays dampened, dimmed, and blocked out" (Jha, 2021). For example, I spend a lot of time writing emails. When doing so, I am directing and holding my flashlight of attention toward my screen while filtering out the many distractions inside and around me: the pings of my imessages, the thoughts in my mind about this morning's meeting, and my stomach signaling that my body needs food. Since I am an adult with intact executive functioning skills, I am able to hone in on composing text, while dampening out other stimuli. Just because I am able to activate my nifty orienting system does not mean it is always easy to use. Our environments are rife with flashlight thieves, often the most egregious ones being inside our own heads – our stinkin' thinkin'!

Alerting System: The Floodlight

Let's consider a classroom example. Most days I would skip my lunch break in order to work on my lesson plans. Considering this example, my orienting system held my flashlight on my laptop while ignoring the sound of the old radiator clicking on and off. My flashlight stayed steady for the precious minutes I had before children began pouring through my door. With some stroke of luck and probably caffeine, I finished preparing my lesson and haphazardly threw math manipulatives on 24 desks, leaving a few moments to sit down, check my phone, then stare out the window in a daze.

As I sat, I noticed a few orange leaves falling to the ground and simultaneously felt sleepy. Since the lesson preparation was complete, my orienting system took a back seat to its sister system, **open awareness**, or the **alerting system**. This attentional system operates more like a floodlight with a wide blanket of light covering inner and outer experiences. The alerting system encompasses a broad awareness, taking in whatever arises: sounds, thoughts, sensations in the body, sights, and more. These "alerts" bubble up through the senses and into the brain where they are evaluated and judged. Is this sound a threat? Is that a snake on the ground or a rope? Is this alert positive, negative, or neutral? Our alerting system has a broad receptive stance, open to whatever arises.

Alerting System at Work!

A teacher sits at his desk grading assignments, his alerting system monitoring the classroom: noticing ambient sounds of students' voices, watching the clock, and hearing his own internal dialogue, *"Ah. Don't forget to check in with Mr. Morales after class about Kamar."*

If, for example, he suddenly sees a bee fly through the opened window, his selective attention (flashlight) takes over, honing in on the bee to eliminate the threat.

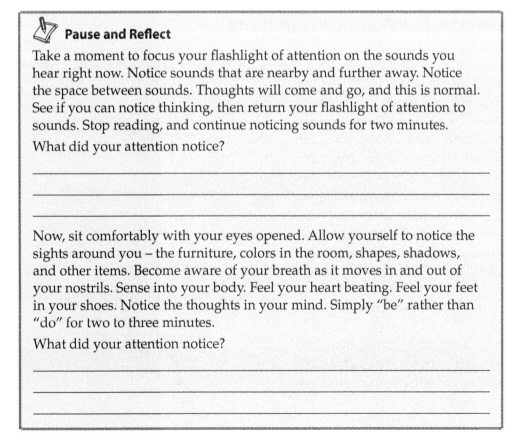

Pause and Reflect

Take a moment to focus your flashlight of attention on the sounds you hear right now. Notice sounds that are nearby and further away. Notice the space between sounds. Thoughts will come and go, and this is normal. See if you can notice thinking, then return your flashlight of attention to sounds. Stop reading, and continue noticing sounds for two minutes.

What did your attention notice?

_____

_____

_____

Now, sit comfortably with your eyes opened. Allow yourself to notice the sights around you – the furniture, colors in the room, shapes, shadows, and other items. Become aware of your breath as it moves in and out of your nostrils. Sense into your body. Feel your heart beating. Feel your feet in your shoes. Notice the thoughts in your mind. Simply "be" rather than "do" for two to three minutes.

What did your attention notice?

_____

_____

_____

Right about now teachers may be wondering why this matters. The truth is that attention is the *bedrock* of teaching and learning. Without it, teaching and learning gravely suffer.

Attentional Control Lays the Foundation for Teaching and Learning

With strong attentional control as the bedrock, executive functions and SEL skills can then be laid and solidified to support the teaching and learning of content.

As teachers, we are facilitators of learning. Therefore, the more we know about how learning works, the more effective our teaching becomes. Educators with a basic understanding of the science of learning make sound decisions for their students, and use science to guide instructional decisions. So, please excuse me while I geek out for a few paragraphs about the human brain. Do not skip this section!

Learning a New Skill: The Role of Attention

To shed light on the connection between attention and learning, let's consider an example. How is it possible that last month my six-year-old daughter Talula had never recognized the word CAN before, but within a few weeks can recognize, pronounce, spell, and write the word CAN correctly? Simply put, the brain is made up of nerve cells called **neurons**. There are approximately 100 billion neurons in the adult brain, each of which is connected to up to 10,000 other neurons. As the brain matures, these networks of neurons become more efficient at doing their job, which is to move chemicals called **neurotransmitters** from neuron to neuron.

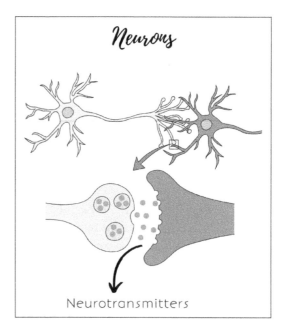

Neurons

Neurotransmitters

Neurons form circuits. The more often a circuit is activated, the deeper it embeds into the folds of the brain, and the faster chemicals flow between neurons. Let's take my daughter decoding the word CAN as an example. When Talula learned to string the phonemes /k/ /a/ /n/ together for the first time, neurons in her brain created a circuit. Each day her brain directed her flashlight of attention to the letters C-A-N strung together, and she practiced correctly decoding the word. Over time, the neurons within the circuit physically moved closer to one another, shrinking the gaps between the neurons. Think of a neural circuit like a racetrack with the rails moving closer and closer together until they lock in place. The rails are the neurons and the cars are the neurotransmitters. With the rails locked together, neurotransmitters flow faster through the circuit.

The more times Talula successfully decoded CAN, the more ingrained that circuit became in her brain. This is an example of neuroplasticity – the brain's ability to physically grow and reorganize itself. If Talula stopped directing her attention to the word CAN, and stopped practicing writing, pronouncing, and spelling CAN, she would likely forget. That's because much like a young sapling, during childhood the brain is actively growing and pruning itself. Whatever neuronal circuits are traveled often become strengthened, while those less traveled go dormant.

My five-year-old boy Zachary loves building elaborate racetracks with those orange and blue Hot Wheels pieces. When he first begins, he doesn't always correctly match up the tongue and groove pieces, and the cars move slowly or fall off the track. This is similar to what happens in our brains when we are learning something new. Once Zachary locks the pieces together and practices with the track, his cars quickly zoom through the track, much like neurotransmitters zipping through their circuits when a new skill is mastered.

Pause and Reflect

As I present information on neuroscience, a topic that may or may not be of interest to you, your attention has wandered multiple times – which is normal. What are you noticing about your ability to sustain and monitor your attention as you read?

_____

_____

_____

Attention + Repeated Practice = Automaticity

Repeated practice of a skill, like decoding, results in what's called **myelination** – the laying down of a protective coating on the axon of neurons. The fatty myelin sheath solidifies the circuit and allows the neurochemicals to efficiently speed through the circuit, resulting in automaticity. Continuing with Talula's reading example, in this stage her brain directs attention to the word CAN, and without hesitation or much "thought" she decodes the word correctly – it is automatic. This experience is vastly different from her initial introduction to the word when she needed to expend a great deal of mental energy to decode the word. The circuit was just forming, therefore her top-down brain controlled the circuit. The top-down brain is responsible for voluntary, detail-oriented thinking and obtaining new information. Top-down processes require a lot of energy, which is why Talula is so tired after a day of learning new things in kindergarten. As decoding CAN reached automaticity with repeated practice, her brain circuit was taken over by bottom-up processing, which is in charge of rote habits and routines. The more circuits controlled by bottom-up processing, the more our attentional system is freed up to learn new things. Whether learning to read or learning to cook a perfect birthday cake, learning requires a great deal of attentional control and skill. Fascinating, am I right?

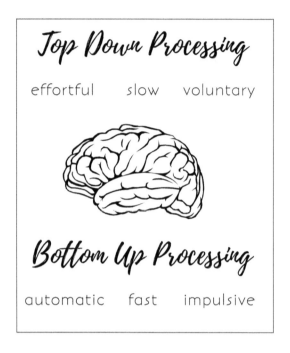

Limitations of Our Current Teaching Strategies

Teachers know that in order for students to learn any new skill from subtracting numerals to sinking a foul shot, they need ample repeated practice. Why then, do we not provide repeated practice in these foundational skills that underlie learning like managing attention, regulating our behaviors, and being present for the moments of our lives?

The opening anecdote about my student, Luke, is one of many in my memory. Over the years, many students in my classroom struggled with attention and self-regulation. I did the best I could with what I knew at the time – implementing basic strategies that I was taught in college and by mentor teachers. Things like providing preferential seating, offering frequent breaks, using standing folders to block out distractions, and redirecting students when off task. Although these strategies can be helpful temporarily, they act more as band aids for the real issue – lack of attentional control. I was never taught *how* to teach students to pay attention, and unfortunately, this remains the case for teachers today.

> **You can have the most well-designed lesson of your week, full of high-tech bells and whistles, but without the ability to maintain, shift, and direct attention, students cannot access the learning we are providing.**

The Current War on Attention

In this day and age, society is in an age of information overload. Our mornings consist of reading world news headlines while fielding text messages from colleagues and shoveling breakfast into our mouths. We are literally drowning in digital input, leading to screen addiction, poor sleep hygiene, and tanking mental health in adults and children like we have never seen before. If we are not taking charge of our attention, our devices will gladly take our seats at the controls. Although it is debatable whether our attention span is actually shrinking, we do know that it has become nearly impossible to concentrate on a single task for any length of time, let alone a string of text that exceeds the length of a tweet. Our children have grown up with iPhones and tablets glued to their palms since toddlerhood. This issue is precisely why the skill of managing attention is so critical in today's world. Many of us feel we are asleep at the wheel, living our lives on autopilot. Luckily, there is a collective waking up and an ever-growing demand for mindful and intentional living. We have the knowledge and volition to change this story, not only for ourselves, but for the rising generations to come.

Teacher Lesson

S.T.O.P.

Teachers must build their attention regulation before guiding students in doing so. If the goal is lasting change, better classroom culture, fewer minutes disciplining students and greater time filled with genuine teaching and learning, teachers must start with themselves.

Over the course of the next hour, day, maybe even week, practice noticing your attention. You might just be surprised by your ability to shift off autopilot and drop into the present moment.

Description: This portable mindful awareness practice trains teachers to direct and sustain attention with a curious and open mind.

Time: 30 seconds.

Frequency: three to five times per day.

S.T.O.P. Practice for Teachers

1. *S – Stop.* Come to a full stop. Put down whatever is in your hands, stop your body, and stand or sit still. You might even picture a stop sign in your mind.
2. *T – Take a Breath.* Feel the expansion of your belly and chest as you fully inhale. Allow the exhale to completely leave the body. Breathe slowly and steadily for two to three breaths.
3. *O – Observe.* Notice your thoughts, emotions, and sensations in your body with curiosity and kindness. No need to change anything – simply notice without judgment.
4. *P – Proceed.* Continue on with your day, taking with you the information you have gained from the S.T.O.P practice.

Tips for Success

♦ Print and cut the provided S.T.O.P. cards to keep handy until you have the steps committed to memory.

♦ Try setting a gentle alarm to sound a few times throughout your day. When the alarm sounds, practice S.T.O.P.

- ◆ Try coupling the S.T.O.P. practice with an established daily habit, like teeth brushing, drinking coffee in the morning, or getting into the car. By attaching a new habit to one that is already embedded in the brain, it can solidify and myelinate faster.
- ◆ Try placing a few of the printed S.T.O.P. signs (provided) around the house and classroom. For example, I have one on my laptop, on my bathroom mirror, and next to the light switch in my office. This visual reminder cues my brain to practice S.T.O.P. a few times per day.

Pause and Reflect

What did you notice about your attention as you practiced? Record any insights below.

_____

_____

_____

Comments from Teachers:

"I never realized how tense my shoulders were all day! Stopping helped me notice the tension and let it go."

"I have been using the S.T.O.P. practice whenever I wash my hands. I usually notice how busy my mind is, thinking of so many to do's."

"Stopping sounds so simple but it's not easy! I feel driven to move at lightning speed through the day."

"I practiced "Stopping" for 2 days, and right away I noticed how distracted I was. While I was walking to the copier I was planning next period's lesson. While I was eating dinner I was catching up on emails. It was really eye opening."

"I found it really hard to just stop, even for 30 seconds. I almost felt guilty letting myself have a moment to not do anything. It made me think about how we are trained to be "productive" at all times."

"Wow. My to-do list is constantly running in my head."

STOP

Description: This practice simply teaches you to notice your attention, without changing or controlling it in any way.
Time: 30 seconds
Frequency: 3-5x per day

Directions:
1. <u>Stop</u> Come to a full stop - put down whatever is in your hands, stop your body, and stand or sit still. You might even picture a stop sign in your mind.
2. <u>Take</u> a breath.
3. <u>Observe</u> Notice your thoughts, the sensations in your body, and any emotions you feel.
4. <u>Proceed</u> Continue on with your day with this new level of awareness.

STOP

Description: This practice simply teaches you to notice your attention, without changing or controlling it in any way.
Time: 30 seconds
Frequency: 3-5x per day

Directions:
1. <u>Stop</u> Come to a full stop - put down whatever is in your hands, stop your body, and stand or sit still. You might even picture a stop sign in your mind.
2. <u>Take</u> a breath.
3. <u>Observe</u> Notice your thoughts, the sensations in your body, and any emotions you feel.
4. <u>Proceed</u> Continue on with your day with this new level of awareness.

STOP

Description: This practice simply teaches you to notice your attention, without changing or controlling it in any way.
Time: 30 seconds
Frequency: 3-5x per day

Directions:
1. <u>Stop</u> Come to a full stop - put down whatever is in your hands, stop your body, and stand or sit still. You might even picture a stop sign in your mind.
2. <u>Take</u> a breath.
3. <u>Observe</u> Notice your thoughts, the sensations in your body, and any emotions you feel.
4. <u>Proceed</u> Continue on with your day with this new level of awareness.

STOP

Description: This practice simply teaches you to notice your attention, without changing or controlling it in any way.
Time: 30 seconds
Frequency: 3-5x per day

Directions:
1. <u>Stop</u> Come to a full stop - put down whatever is in your hands, stop your body, and stand or sit still. You might even picture a stop sign in your mind.
2. <u>Take</u> a breath.
3. <u>Observe</u> Notice your thoughts, the sensations in your body, and any emotions you feel.
4. <u>Proceed</u> Continue on with your day with this new level of awareness.

Five-Minute Student Microlesson

Taking Charge of Attention
This microlesson is written for students aged 5–10. See notes for use with older students.

Concepts
Teachers introduce the concept that attention is like a flashlight in the brain, emphasizing that students are in charge of their own flashlights of attention. This is important because being in charge of the flashlight of attention makes schoolwork, homework, and learning new things easier!

Delivery
Hook: Teacher drops a book – creating a loud noise. Students look. T*: "What just happened" S*: "You dropped a book." "You made a loud sound." T: "Yes, when I dropped the book many of you looked. The sound caught your *attention*. But what does it mean to pay attention? Turn and talk to share ideas."

Demonstrate: T: "Your attention is like a flashlight in your brain. You are in charge of where you direct (point) your flashlight of attention. Being in charge of your flashlight of attention makes schoolwork, homework, and learning new things easier!"

Participate: Teacher asks students to point attention to various objects around the room: different words on the bulletin boards, stapler on teacher's desk, etc. T: "Notice how you are in charge of where you point your flashlight of attention, and how long you hold it there."

Thread: T: "Today during class, I will stop and ask you to notice where you are directing your flashlight of attention. See if you can notice for yourself where your attention is pointed while you complete your classwork."

Model: *(examples)*

T: "Right now I'm focusing my flashlight of attention on Xavier as he reads his story aloud."

T: "I'm noticing that my flashlight of attention is focused on the words I'm reading, and my brain is thinking about the meaning."

T: "My flashlight keeps shifting to the loudspeaker as we are getting interrupted with announcements. Where is your flashlight? Turn and tell your desk partners."

T: "Laser beams on the white board as I demonstrate how to solve for X."

*T: indicates teacher speech
*S: indicates student speech

Lesson, Differentiation, Modifications, and Notes

Trauma-Informed: Keep the lesson accessible and equitable by having extra flashlights on hand if requested from home (see notes below). Keep in mind that students with a history of trauma may be more easily startled, so choose the loud noise wisely.

Neurodivergent: Students diagnosed with ADD/ADHD may have underlying beliefs about their ability to manage attention. Teachers may mention that some brains have an easier time controlling the flashlight than others, and that is normal. Students with disabilities (SWD) may benefit from partnering with neurotypical peers during turn and talk.

English Learners: Consider removing idioms from instruction (e.g., caught your attention). Idioms and analogies can be challenging for English learners, therefore it may be helpful to introduce the term "flashlight of attention" in students' native language before introducing the English terms.

Gifted Learners: Ask students to summarize the concepts and create a visual, or help teach those who were absent or need a reminder.

Notes:

★ Middle and high school teachers have used words like "laser beam" to describe attention. When asking older students to *participate* in shifting their attention, teachers might suggest subtle places like the soles of the feet or sensations of clothing.

★ Younger students (K–2) may benefit from an actual flashlight being used for demonstration purposes. Some elementary teachers have allowed students to bring flashlights from home. Other teachers have pretended to hold a flashlight when cuing the skill by placing a fist, knuckles up, next to their head. Students then copy this gesture.

★ Remember, the goal of the hook is to use novelty to gain students' attention. Over the years I have seen teachers create some excellent hooks for this lesson, including:

    playing loud dance party music as students enter the classroom/gymnasium;

    wearing a clown nose as teacher greet students;

    spilling a jar of marbles onto the floor.

★ See Online Support Materials for sample lessons that have been adapted for various grade levels and learning environments.

Tips for Success

- ♦ Bring the abstract concept of paying attention to students by explicitly choosing your words: e.g., "point your flashlight of attention toward…" vs. arbitrarily saying "pay attention to…"
- ♦ Keep the pace brisk and intentional – this microlesson should take no longer than five to seven minutes. Teach the microlesson *before* beginning to teach other content. Thread the concept through subsequent lessons (i.e., math, social studies) throughout the day by modeling the skill.
- ♦ The microlessons come alive through modeling and cueing the skills. When teachers fail to model the skill, the learning cannot deeply embed into the folds of the brain.
- ♦ Once taught, teachers may continue to thread and model the skill in the days that follow. Be sure to provide ample repeated practice before moving on to the next microlesson.

Comments from Teachers:

"I taught the flashlight microlesson to my class and have been using it as a way to get their attention before a lesson/giving direction. It's been helpful, students have started making gestures and sounds like they are turning on a flashlight. I want to keep embedding it into the day, especially to help students refocus on their independent work."

Plan for Success

How and when might you implement this concept? What spaces in the day might you use? Who might you call on for support/ideas? How might you handle potential roadblocks?

_____
_____
_____
_____
_____

Post-Teaching Reflection

What would you add or change? What worked and what didn't? What did your attention notice?

_____

_____

_____

_____

_____

Reference

Jha, A. (2021). *Peak mind*. HarperCollins.

3

The Lie

Some Students Cannot Pay Attention

The Truth: All students can build foundational skills, including attention management, with explicit instruction.

 Key Concepts in This Chapter:

★ A lack of foundational skills may negatively affect teachers' decisions, resulting in demoralization and burnout.
★ Developing foundational skills allow teachers to uncover unconscious beliefs, biases, and assumptions that may or may not be true.
★ A teacher's understanding of neuroplasticity affects how and what content is taught, in turn affecting student outcomes.
★ Attention deficit hyperactivity disorder (ADHD) is a breakdown or underdevelopment of foundational skills.
★ Attention management supports executive functioning and SEL skills. Without attentional control, EF and SEL skills suffer.

The Teacher's Pet and the Struggling Student

I have devoted my entire career to education, in part because I loved being a student myself. As a young child, I was always the so-called teacher's pet. In

DOI: 10.4324/9781003316275-3

fact, my first-grade teacher had always put me in charge of helping the substitutes when she was absent. As a healthy, neurotypical learner coming from
a family of teachers, I had little trouble learning to read, write, and remain
seated in my chair. I paid attention, followed directions, and kept track of
my materials. Oftentimes, my elementary school teachers sat struggling students nearby so I could model "positive" student behaviors. I remember one
particular student, Chris, who was seated next to me in second grade. I often
watched Chris as he played inside his desk, stared out the window, or picked
his ear while the teacher was reading.

As entertaining as it is to remember my elementary school days, I can't
help but realize how students like Chris lacked the foundational skills
needed for learning. The classroom teacher intervened as best she could,
but Chris's behavior remained the same. Life came full circle when I,
myself, was in her shoes about 20 years later, unsure of how to help my
own struggling students.

Pause and Reflect

What do you remember about yourself as a young learner? In what ways
did your early experiences with schooling influence your career choices?

_____

_____

_____

When Foundational Skills Are Absent in Teachers or Students

I waltzed into my first job like I knew everything there was to know about
teaching. I had a Master's degree in Special Education and graduated with
high honors. I had fresh-out-of-college innovative ideas that would help students learn and thrive. There I went to save the children – or so I thought.
Unfortunately, my enthusiasm was quickly crushed when I received the
message from veteran teachers that we "teach what's in the manual" and
"non-tenured staff don't say anything," at all – about anything ... ever. My
innovative ideas were sadly cast aside as I struggled to assimilate to the reality of public-school education.

After a few short months it became clear that my co-teacher, the general
educator, was in charge of the curricular decisions while I was expected to
work with "my students" – the students with Individualized Education Plans

(IEPs). "My students" never had pencils, kept the messiest bookbags, struggled to read for meaning, and certainly could not pay attention or regulate their behaviors without assistance.

Though this segregation of the class felt morally wrong and was against the inclusive education practices I had learned, I tried my best to acquiesce and not rock the boat. I disagreed with many of my co-teacher's decisions, which left me feeling stressed and morally conflicted. I did not agree with teaching geometry lessons 14.5 on Monday, 14.6 on Tuesday, and 14.7 on Wednesday because by Thursday many students were still struggling to master Monday's lesson. It was my first taste of feeling demoralized. This position was not sustainable – I was forced to bite my tongue and concede to my co-teacher just because he was a tenured staff member. If I had stronger foundational skills myself, it's possible I might have voiced my concerns, managed my emotions, and solved the problem.

Uncovering Lies I Believed

No matter what I tried, some students just could not stay focused. I started to think that maybe some students simply *could not pay attention*. Rather than questioning my methods or reflecting on my toolbox of strategies, I began to point the finger at my students. I started viewing them through the lens of their deficits, rather than through the lens of their strengths. I believed that certain children lacked attention, therefore attention must be fixed and unchangeable. Students had the ability to manage attention or not. It was like being born with blue eyes or blonde hair – they either had it or simply didn't. I wish I knew then what I know now – that these foundational skills are trainable, and that focusing on what students *can't* do doesn't work.

I felt confident teaching three ways of solving a math problem, but I struggled to find effective strategies to explicitly teach the foundational skills the students so desperately needed. Skills like inhibition – how to resist the urge to talk during quizzes, or task monitoring – checking comprehension while reading.

Looking back, it is hard not to feel terribly guilty for failing to teach my students how to pay attention, stay on task, manage their thoughts and be more successful learners. Since then, I have spent years immersing myself in training, research, and experience to develop and perfect my ability to teach foundational skills to teachers and students. My drive to raise awareness of the importance of these skills has fueled my work with thousands of teachers across the world, positively influencing millions of students.

> **Pause and Reflect**
>
> What strategies do you currently use to help students pay attention? Do they work? How do you know?
>
> _____
>
> _____
>
> _____

Teachers: Growers and Re-organizers of Student Brains

Human brains reorganize themselves in response to experience. This phenomenon, known as **neuroplasticity**, is important to understand since it affects the way we conceptualize learning and how we view our students' abilities. Teachers who provide rich learning experiences literally rewire young brain matter. Dr. Carol Dweck's work in growth mindset is based on the science of neuroplasticity, and teaches us that "test scores and measures of achievement tell you where a student is, but they don't tell you where a student could end up" (Dweck, 2016). Just as teachers explicitly teach algebra, French, Latin, and robotics – they can teach the foundational skills of attentional control, executive functioning, and SEL. This is not to suggest that all students have the same capacity to master these skills. Neuroscience research has revealed that although all brains are capable of growth and change, "no two brains have the same anatomy" (Valizadeh et al., 2018).

Attention Deficit Hyperactivity Disorder – A Breakdown of Foundational Skills

I have taught, tutored, and coached many students diagnosed with attention deficit hyperactivity disorder (ADHD), both with and without hyperactivity, and no two students were alike. I taught a fourth-grader named Kate*, who struggled to comprehend what she read. After being diagnosed with ADHD mid-year, she began avoiding all of her reading assignments. For Kate, the diagnosis implied that she no longer had to complete assignments that felt challenging. Her faulty belief, whether conscious or not, negatively affected

---

* All names have been changed.

her performance. Had her foundational skill of **self-awareness** been better developed, she may have been able to confront this belief and change her behavior. I taught a middle schooler, Luca, who impulsively called out while the teacher was talking. Luca would have benefitted from explicit instruction in **inhibition**. Griffin, in second grade, procrastinated for 30 minutes before beginning his classwork, but had no problem maintaining concentration once he finally began. **Task initiation**, an essential element of executive functioning, needed to be practiced.

A diagnosis is not a recipe for how to best teach a student. "ADHD itself is a disorder of executive function" (Bertin, 2018), which is precisely why no single teaching strategy, behavior modification chart, or intervention works for all students. Executive functions underlie learning by monitoring our thinking and behavior. Developing around age two, EF skills do not fully mature until around age 30. When a student enters a classroom with a diagnosis, label, exceptionality, or IEP, it is an alert urging the teacher to lean in and get curious. Spending time getting to know each student helps teachers identify which attentional, executive, or social-emotional skills to target for remediation.

A Closer Look at Foundational Skills

SEL Skill	Function in a School Setting (Example)	Dysfunction in a School Setting (Example)
Self-awareness	Noticing feelings of frustration during a challenging subject	Difficulty noticing and naming emotions; unable to explain why one acts out
Self-management	Setting goals to complete a multi-step project, then executing	Struggling to organize thoughts and materials
Social Awareness	Adjusting behavior to match different teachers' expectations	Inability to empathize with other students' perspectives
Responsible Decision Making	Completing group work in a timely fashion, with care and concern for the collective grade	Acting on one's own behalf, without forethought of how behaviors and actions affect others
Relationship Skills	Developing and maintaining peer friendships	Difficulty working in pairs or groups; showing rigidity

Executive Functioning Skill	Function in a School Setting (Example)	Dysfunction in a School Setting (Example)
Working Memory	Recalling key details like setting, characters, and time period after reading a text	Forgetting two of the three verbal directions given by the teacher
Task Monitoring	Noticing when comprehension has broken down and applying a strategy like rereading, reading on, or asking a question	Spending most of the class period deciding on a writing topic rather than creating the outline due at the end of the period
Task Initiation	Entering the classroom, unpacking, and getting started on morning work without prompting from teacher	Wandering the room, staring at a blank page, and struggling to get started on tasks
Planning	Successfully filling-in a Venn diagram and utilizing it to write an essay	Writing a free flow of thoughts with no clear beginning, middle, or end
Organizing	Mentally rehearsing talking points to share during a small group book talk	Raising a hand to answer a question before knowing the answer
Time Management	Pacing oneself to finish a project or assessment	Belaboring one element of an assignment leaving little time for remaining sections
Behavioral Monitoring	Remaining focused while feeling hungry, tired, or restless	Calling out, interrupting
Inhibition	Diligently staying on task while others talk and goof off	Struggling to keep hands to oneself
Problem Solving	Applying multiple strategies to decode an unknown word	Becoming "stuck" and giving up

Attentional Control Skill	Function in a School Setting (Example)	Dysfunction in a School Setting (Example)
Orienting	Sustaining attention to an assignment while ignoring background noise	Trouble staying on task during student-directed work, easily distracted
Alerting	Considering peer comments during class discussions; listening to others	Missing verbal directions from teacher, hyperfocusing, seemingly in "own world"

> **Pause and Reflect**
>
> What background knowledge do you have about foundational skills: attentional control, executive functioning, and social-emotional learning? Which students came to mind when reviewing the examples of dysfunction?
>
> _____
>
> _____
>
> _____

Attentional Control – Begin with the Bedrock

Without a strong foundation in attentional control, executive and SEL skills suffer. This is why it is critical to begin with molding and shaping students' attention. Unfortunately, many widely adopted SEL and character education curricula omit this critical skill set. Teaching a middle school student how to monitor his comprehension while reading is not effective without first teaching him how to notice when he is distracted. Similarly, attempting to teach a student social skills like developing empathy and perspective taking first requires paying attention to one's own thoughts and emotions.

Teacher Lesson

Counting Breaths

Counting breaths is a simple mindfulness practice that helps develop attention management. Record yourself reading the Counting Breaths script then play it back, or access a guided practice at www.rootsandwingsonline.org.

> **Pause and Reflect**
>
> What are your expectations as you begin a new mindfulness practice? If you have experimented with formal mindfulness practices in the past, record your insights here.
>
> _____
>
> _____
>
> _____

Contrary to popular belief portrayed in the media, the goal of mindfulness practice is **not** to become calm and happy, but rather to notice human experience in the moment with kindness and curiosity. Instead of attempting to change or reject whatever may be happening in the moment, try welcoming each moment-by-moment experience with gentleness and compassion.

Counting Breaths

Find a comfortable seated posture. Place your feet flat on the floor, if that feels comfortable. You may choose to close your eyes or keep your eyes downcast toward the floor with a soft gaze. You might place your hands in your lap either palms up or palms down. Take a moment to focus your flashlight of attention on the sounds around you. Settle into your seat, and know that the purpose of this practice is to simply experience the present moments of your life.

Next, shift your attention to the tip of your nostrils and notice the sensations of your breath. Take a long, slow, deep inhale, drawing the breath into your abdomen. Repeat for three cycles, then return to your natural breath, keeping your attention on the nostrils. You will notice many distractions: sounds, thoughts, sensations in your body, possibly even emotions. Allow your attention to touch on each distraction, then gently shift your flashlight to the next sensation of breath.

Inhale and exhale, silently noting *one*, counting your breath. Again, inhale, exhale, count *two*. See if you can continue counting to ten breaths. If you become lost in thought, distracted or sleepy, begin again. Hold yourself with kindness and be curious about this practice. Stop at ten breaths, or when you reach seven to ten minutes of practice.

Tips for Success

♦ Find seven to ten minutes daily to practice Counting Breaths to strengthen your attention management skills. Many teachers use this practice first thing in the morning upon waking, or just before bed at night. Others close their classroom doors and use five minutes of their prep period to practice Counting Breaths.

♦ To help work this into your day, it may be helpful to link this practice with a habit you already have, such as making coffee or brushing your teeth. Many teachers sit at their kitchen tables practicing mindfulness while their coffee brews!

♦ It is normal to notice many thoughts in the mind and become distracted from the breath. This is part of the practice!

◆ If at any time during this practice you feel unsafe, anxious, or dizzy please listen to your body's signals and stop the practice. Try again with some modifications, like keeping your eyes open, standing up, or shortening the length of practice.

Pause and Reflect

What did your attention notice during the Counting Breaths practice?

_____

_____

_____

Five-Minute Student Microlesson

Strengthening Attention

This microlesson is designed for students aged 7–12. See notes and online support materials for older and younger students.

Concepts

Students learn that it is possible to strengthen attention by practicing.

Delivery

Hook: Standing Survey: Teacher asks a series of –three to five questions and students stand to indicate a "yes" response. T: "Stand if you play a sport like soccer, basketball, or tennis." *Students stand then sit.* Stand if you know how to read chapter books. Stand if you know how to cook. T: "How did you get better at playing sports? How did you get better at reading? How did you get better at building Lego towers?" Allow students to share their responses. Lead students to concluding that it took *practice*.

Demonstrate: T: "Does anyone ever notice themselves starting to wander during long presentations, or while reading a book that feels boring to them? This means it's sometimes hard to pay attention. But good news! We can get better at paying attention by using mindfulness strategies. Mindfulness means noticing what's happening now. It is being in charge of your flashlight. Let me show you how this works." Teacher models Counting Breaths Mindfulness Practice using the supplied handout.

Participate: Students review Counting Breaths handout and practice. T: "What did your attention notice?"

Thread: T: "Today during class, we might stop and complete a round of Counting Breaths to help us practice paying attention."

Model: *(examples)*

T: "As I'm focusing my flashlight of attention, I'm feeling the air flowing into my nose, then breathing out and letting it go."

T: "My attention is noticing that as I'm tracing my circles, I'm distracted by the sounds in the room. That's okay! I notice the sounds from the hallway, and direct my flashlight back to my job."

T: "As I'm reading in my head, I'm practicing keeping my flashlight of attention on my job, just like when we were Counting Breaths."

Plan for Success

How and when might you implement this concept? What spaces in the day might you use? Who might you call on for support/ideas? How might you handle potential roadblocks?

_____

_____

_____

Post-Teaching Reflection

What would you add or change? What worked and what didn't? What did your attention notice?

_____

_____

_____

Reflection from a first-grade teacher:

"While teaching the lesson I thought it was a good idea to use exaggerated breaths and a large circle in the air with a finger tracing around it. Students practiced using this method and really enjoyed it. They definitely understood the concept of losing your focus and taking breaths to bring it back to learning. However, one thing that I noticed through teaching the lesson was that I needed to transition to teaching students to take "circle breaths" without being a distraction to the other kids. They could do this by making a circle in their palm or on their leg and they also didn't have to use an exaggerated breath. They could simply breathe through their noses. Once I taught them how, I noticed students practicing on their own throughout the day."

Lesson Differentiation, Modifications, and Notes

Trauma-Informed: Growing up with limited resources or lack of parental involvement limits students' exposure to common childhood skills like bike riding, swimming, and gaming. Be sure to include basic skills (e.g., brushing teeth, hopping, running) during the hook to allow all students to participate.

Neurodivergent: Students who struggle with attention management may begin by practicing five breaths rather than ten. Those who are sensory avoidant sometimes prefer tracing circles with a pen or the eraser of a pencil rather than touching finger to paper, while those who are sensory seeking may benefit from Counting Breaths printed on heavyweight or textured paper. Some students with disabilities (SWD) may benefit from using gross motor movements like circling the arms while inhaling and exhaling.

English Learners: Consider providing a translated copy of Counting Breaths for at-home practice. Pre-teach new vocabulary: sensations, mindfulness.

Gifted Learners: Normalize the fact that students who are classified as gifted or advanced track may not also be gifted in the domains of attention management, executive functioning, and social-emotional learning skills.

Notes:

★ *Hook* modifications

Lower grades: Stand if you like to play Minecraft. Stand if you can ride a bike. Stand if you can write your name.

Middle and upper grades: Stand if you use social media. Stand if you can multiply fractions. Stand if you can say hello in more than one language.

★ Counting Breaths may be laminated and placed in students' desks or folders for ease of use as a Do-Now or brain break.

★ *Participate* modifications

Lower grades: K–3 students may benefit from practicing Counting Breaths with their fingers tracing invisible circles in the air, or with a variety of textures like sand or shaving cream on cookie sheets. Or, students may benefit from using the modified sheet so as not to be distracted by too much text.

★ Once students are accustomed to the Counting Breaths practice, it can easily be transferred to a single circle on an index card or even a quarter or button.

Counting Breaths

Mindfulness Practice

Counting Breaths may help manage *stress*, increase focus, and promote a healthy body and mind.

• • • • • • • • • • •

1. Stop what you are doing and find a comfortable seated position with your feet flat on the floor.

2. Place your finger on the star at the top of circle 1. Breathe in through your *nose* while tracing the outline of the circle, stopping at the dot. Feel the sensations at your nostrils.

3. Breathe out through your nose while tracing from the dot back up to the star.

4. Repeat steps 1-3 with Circles 2-10: inhale from star to dot, exhale from dot to star, fully tracing each circle with each breath. Focus your flashlight of attention on your nostrils.

See if you can focus all of your attention on the *sensations* of the breath as it moves through your nose, into your lungs, and back out. Each time your attention notices a sound, a thought, or another distraction, gently move your flashlight of attention back to the *sensations* of your breath.

Counting Breaths

Mindfulness Practice

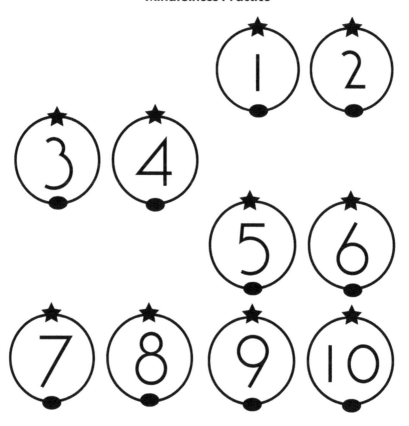

Modified Sheet

References

Bertin, M. (2018). *How Children Thrive: The Practical Science of Raising Independent, Resilient, and Happy Kids*. Sounds True.

Dweck, C. (2016). *Mindset: The new psychology of success*. Ballantine Books.

Valizadeh, S. A., Liem, F., Mérillat, S., Hänggi, J., & Jäncke, L. (2018). Identification of individual subjects on the basis of their brain anatomical features. *Scientific Reports*, *8*(1). DOI: 10.1038/s41598-018-23696-6.

4

The Lie

This Job Doesn't Afford Me the Time or Resources Needed for Adequate Self-Care

The Truth: Self-care: it's not what you think.

 Key Concepts in This Chapter:
★ Self-care need not be elaborate, expensive, or shameful.
★ Teacher self-care is not the answer to systemic failures in education.
★ Burnout and demoralization are two related, yet separate challenges teachers face.
★ Teacher SEL is paramount to education reform.

"I know I need a mental health day but it actually adds more stress. It takes forever to plan and then the whole day I'm worried about who is with my kids and if I remembered everything. I have the added guilt that my colleagues lost their preps because I took off and there are no substitutes." – Kindergarten teacher

Misconceptions about the What and How of Self-Care

A few years ago, I purchased an old house in foreclosure. It was a complete disaster, yet full of potential. Even though I was not the one who built the house, I inherited its creaky floors and shoddy windows, and became

DOI: 10.4324/9781003316275-4

responsible for its repair, upkeep, and renovation. The American education system is like an old house in foreclosure. The teachers who are willing to roll up their sleeves and dig into renovations have endless possibilities and potential ahead. However, in order to be a successful participant on the renovations team, teachers must commit to caring for themselves *first.*

As a classroom teacher, I viewed eating breakfast or lunch while actually sitting down as an anomaly. I believed that I could not allow myself to hit the pause button, breathe, or stop even for a moment or else the sky may fall. The thoughts sounded something like this:

◆ "I can't relax right now because I have too much to get done."
◆ "Take a minute for myself? Yeah, I wish!"
◆ "I just have to keep going no matter what."
◆ "I'm doing it for the kids."

Relatable? I know.

If I somehow managed to carve out a tiny slice of time for myself, I was met with a wave of guilt and unworthiness. I could not even enjoy my once-a-year manicure without feeling undeserving. I thought "I should be grading… planning… working… rather than taking a minute for myself." This is **cognitive dissonance**. It occurs when beliefs do not match behavior, and it creates more stress. Isn't it ironic that the manicure, a self-care activity I chose to help refresh and relax me, had done the opposite? Educators are so used to operating in a state of fight or flight that down-shifting their nervous systems seems scary and uncomfortable.

I believed the lie that my job did not afford me the time or resources needed for adequate self-care, and then proceeded to work myself into the ground. I believed that in order to "count" as self-care, it had to involve someone massaging my shoulders. This narrow understanding of self-care practices hindered my mental and physical health, which in turn affected my teaching. It is clear to me now that there are numerous self-care activities that don't involve a spa trip.

Pause and Reflect

Record your beliefs about self-care. Then, list some ways you care for yourself.

_____

_____

_____

Sample Self-Care "Unroutine"

Our society values productivity over all else, leading to the belief that it is unacceptable to pause even for a moment, let alone actually rest. I continue to combat society's messaging around stress management by reminding myself that caring for *me* is an absolute essential part of daily life. Taking the time to tend to my emotions, regulate my behavior, and reflect on my thoughts helps me to be the teacher, mother, and colleague I want to be. Here is my list of simple self-care practices that I sprinkle into my day-to-day life in order to help me rejuvenate, ground, and re-humanize.

- reading a book unrelated to work;
- setting a timer to engage in the STOP practice multiple times per day (see Chapter 2);
- drinking water;
- sleeping for at least seven hours per night;
- spending a few minutes per day in nature;
- stretching my muscles;
- playing with my children without distraction.

None of these self-care practices happen routinely enough to be deemed *habits* which is totally okay. In fact, I have learned that the best self-care I can practice is *giving myself grace*. I try to remember that life is unpredictable and uncertain, and that a little gentleness goes a long way.

Pause and Reflect

What makes you feel calm, grounded, and like your best self? Unsure? List a few ideas to try. For suggestions, see The Tree of Contemplative Practices, (CMIND, 2021) found at https://www.contemplativemind.org/practices/tree.

_____

_____

_____

Disentangling Teacher Self-Care from School Failures

Last week I emailed one of my principals an agenda to review for her staff's upcoming professional development. She and I have developed a great working relationship over the years, and are often very open with one another. She responded, "Can you cut out the _breathing thing_ and just focus on the strategies for students? It annoys the teachers." My first reaction was a twang of anxiety in my stomach. I felt offended and annoyed that the teachers complained about the three minutes of mindfulness I often used to begin the training. Pausing for a beat allowed me to process my thoughts and emotions and shift into the teachers' perspective. I immediately felt my annoyance dissipate into a swell of compassion in my chest. It dawned on me that asking teachers to pause and breathe before hitting them with what felt like _another professional development_ that they did not want might feel insulting or infantilizing. Many teachers are turned off by professional development sessions about mindfulness, wellness, or self-care because they are so tapped out by the demands of their jobs that these workshops feel patronizing. One teacher said this to me:

> "We don't want the ice cream truck, we just want fewer meetings that could have been emails."

The wellness economy has grown exponentially in the last decade, most notably in the post-COVID years with a current value of 52.5 billion in the United States alone (www.globalwellnessinstitute.org). _Wellthy_ is the new healthy, and healthy is the new wealthy. While I agree that preventative care of my body and mind is important, I disagree with the way self-care is being weaponized, specifically in education, as a cure-all for a deteriorating system.

Self-care, mindfulness, and resilience training have been handed to teachers in response to valid job-related concerns – which is wrong. Don't have enough training in the new math curriculum? Go take a bath! Struggling with student behavior? Develop some grit. Squeeze in a yoga class! Conflicts with a supervisor? Get some exercise or go buy a new journal!

Teachers don't need more *grit*, they need more *help*. Blaming teachers for their lack of self-care or low resilience is yet another way educators are faulted for something out of their control – an oppressive work environment. Teachers cannot continue to operate in an antiquated system with administrators that devalue their skills and negate their requests. Would they benefit from some mindfulness practices and a girls' night out? Probably. However, no amount of breathing or happy hours are going to ameliorate the very real systemic challenges teachers face.

Exhaustion and Burnout: Not Our Fault, but Our Challenge to Overcome

When the powers that be respond to teachers' concerns with "you need to take better care of yourself," **teachers believe the lie that it is their fault that they are struggling, exhausted, and ready to quit.** This could not be further from the truth. "When the demands of the situation overwhelm the available resources, teachers become emotionally exhausted and give up" (Jennings, 2020). It has taken many years for the education system to reach crisis level, to no fault of its teachers. Nevertheless, this is the system we have inherited.

Burnout vs. Demoralization

Working in a Philadelphia charter school for children in foster care led to periods of intense burnout. I remember numerous grueling administrative meetings, where we were constantly stressing about our chronically truant students. In order to renew the charter for another year, nearly 50 students needed to come to school and take the Measures of Academic Progress (MAP) test before the deadline. I remember our security guard ended up driving around the city picking up students off the street corners, bringing them breakfast and convincing them to come to school. I remember the day I had to break up a hair-pulling screaming match between two irate girls, one of which was pregnant. I remember spending many nights worrying about unhomed students. But the night I remember the most vividly is when I got the call that one of my students lost his life to gun violence.

Every morning I stepped through the metal detectors at the charter school with my guard up – anxious, and ready for battle. Being in a constant state of chronic stress affected every area of my life, professionally and personally. Often, I found myself escaping into overeating or overworking to avoid intense emotions like overwhelm, helplessness, and fatigue. It was easier to drink wine and check out than allow myself to experience the despair I felt from seeing students I loved get shuffled from home to home with their garbage bags of belongings in hand. I was not only burning out, I was morally conflicted. I knew what my students needed: social-emotional learning, intense academic intervention, and a group of consistent caring educators with whom to bond. Unfortunately, providing these interventions was nearly impossible. Doris Santoro's book, *Demoralized* (2018), perfectly captures my experience during those years in Philadelphia. "Demoralization is rooted in discouragement and despair borne out of ongoing value conflicts with pedagogical policies, reform mandates, and school practices" (p. 3). Whereas a burned-out teacher is blamed for lacking resilience and accused of not being "gritty enough," a demoralized teacher is seen as a product of the environment at large.

When teachers feel burned out the intervention includes self-care and other support. When teachers are experiencing demoralization, it is an indication that the school context needs reform. Re-moralizing ourselves, according to Santoro, involves engaging with a professional community, identifying allies, stepping into positions of leadership, and engaging in activism (p. 117).

The trend of teacher demoralization leads to chronic attrition. It points to the real issues in the ecosystems of our schools – the lack of proper training and support, initiative overload, overcrowded classrooms, and inequities among teaching staff.

Teacher SEL as a Precedent to Education Reform

In her book *Teacher Burnout Turnaround* (2020), Dr. Patricia Jennings discusses how educators are uniquely positioned to lead educational reform, from the inside out. "I'm certain that with empowerment and will, this transformation process can and must begin in individual classrooms, schools, and districts with individually empowered educators, students, and parents leading the way" (p. 18). When educators are exhausted, demoralized, and operating

Table 4.1 Burnout vs. Demoralization

	Example	Interventions
Burnout	Chronic stress; fatigue; lack of motivation to continue teaching	Time and space for self-care; boundaries between work and home
Demoralization	Being forced to teach in ways known to be ineffective; lack of voice in decision making; feeling stuck and unsupported	Stepping into positions of leadership; aligning with like-minded colleagues; engaging in activism

from survival mode, they cannot engage in educational reform. Santoro (2018) notes that it may be time for teachers to consider *pushing back* rather than *bouncing back*. To do so begins with shifting away from teacher martyrdom, working around the clock, and crafting Pinterest-worthy bulletin boards and toward setting boundaries, tuning in with the body, and shifting attention to the inner self.

Teacher Lesson

Oxygen Masks

One of the ways that teachers can engage in simple self-care is by connecting with their physical bodies. Humans spend their lives focusing on thoughts of the past or future, and are rarely ever truly present. Teachers live as though their bodies are simply transportation for their brains, spending days and nights thinking, planning, and ruminating. The body, with its sensations, emotions, changing states of warmth and coolness, hunger and satiety, is *always* present. Take a moment to consider your relationship with your body. As you reflect on the following questions, try to remain open and curious. Pause and notice if your jaw clenches or you begin to hold your breath. This is a practice of allowing whatever is in your mind to flow freely onto the page.

> **Pause and Reflect**
>
> How do you treat your body when it is sick or tired?
>
> Do you use sick and personal days? Why or why not?
>
> How do you nourish your body? (foods/water/daylight/exercise)
>
> How do you respond when your body gets hurt?
>
> Do you notice signals from your body, such as requests for food, need to use the bathroom, etc.
>
> _____
>
> _____
>
> _____
>
> _____
>
> _____
>
> Next, read over what you wrote and underline/highlight what stands out. Record any insights here: _____
>
> _____

Notice

Notice if you feel guilt, shame or any other emotion. What does it feel like? Where do you feel it?

_____

_____

Reflections from teachers:

> *"Wow… I am really hard on myself."*
> *"I don't ever let myself off the hook."*
> *"I'm always in go mode."*
> *"I never make time for myself."*

Note: The following lessons introduce a mindfulness practice called the body scan. Be conscious that individuals with a history of trauma may feel unsafe placing attention in various parts of the body. Always invite yourself or your students to focus attention on the breath or the soles of the feet when feelings of unease or anxiety arise. All mindfulness practices are an invitation – not a requirement. Students are always welcome to sit quietly and observe rather than participate.

Teacher Practice: Body Scan

Set aside ten minutes before bed to practice the body scan. You can record yourself reading the following script then play it back, or find a guided practice at www.rootsandwingsonline.org.

You can also record yourself reading the following script, then play it back.

Body Scan Practice

Sit down at your desk, turning your chair away from your computer. Take a few deep breaths in through the nose and out through the nose. You might close your eyes or keep them downcast. Imagine that your attention is like a flashlight in your brain, and you are responsible for where you direct your flashlight. Shift your attention to the sensations of your breath at the tip of your nostrils. Notice the temperatures as the air flows in and out of the nose. If there are parts of your body that feel unsafe or triggering, come back to your breath as your home base. Now shift your flashlight to the sensations at the top of your head. Notice any tingling or temperatures in your scalp. With your next breath, move your attention down your face, sensing the head and neck, then the upper back and shoulders. Notice any tingling or tension as you inhale and exhale. Now move your flashlight of attention down your torso and arms, sensing into the hands and fingers. Notice thoughts coming and going in your mind. No need to push them away – just simply notice and label them – *thinking*, then shift your attention back to the body. Continue shifting the attention down your body, keeping an attitude of openness and curiosity. As you end with your attention in your feet, deepen the breath for a few cycles, then rest in gratitude for this amazing, living, breathing body that you are so privileged to inhabit.

Tips for Success

- ◆ Practice the body scan once a week to get accustomed to *being* rather than constantly *doing*.
- ◆ Feeling sleepy during the body scan is normal.
- ◆ Many people enjoy the body scan lying down before bed.
- ◆ Try incorporating mini body scans throughout the day (e.g., when washing your hands, entering or leaving your classroom).
- ◆ Set an alarm on your phone as a reminder to practice shifting your attention into your body.

Five-Minute Student Microlesson

Body Scan

This microlesson is designed for all ages; however, notes are provided to include more scientific terms for older students. See additional differentiated lessons in the online support materials.

Concepts

Students practice shifting attention around the body by engaging their orienting system.

Delivery

Hook: T: "Today we will shift our attention into our bodies. Place your hand over your heart. Notice your heart rate. Notice your breath."
Choose a quick one-minute practice that raises students' heart rates. Examples: Jogging in place, 30 jumping jacks, wall sits, etc.

Demonstrate: T: "Place your hand over your heart again. Put your flashlight of attention on your chest. Notice your breath. What's happening with your heartbeat? Turn and talk to your neighbor to share what your flashlight of attention notices." *Students turn and talk to share then the teacher calls on one or two students to share aloud.*

Participate: T: "We don't pay much attention to our bodies because our flashlights are always stuck shining on our thoughts! However, our bodies communicate information, like telling us when we are hungry, tired, worried, in pain, and more. Let's practice shifting our flashlight of attention off of our busy minds and into our bodies now." Teacher chooses a sample body scan script from the included examples. End by asking students how they are feeling after a brief body scan.

Thread: T: "As we switch from class to class, we will pause and shift our flashlights of attention into our bodies to check in."

Model: *(examples)*

T: "We have 20 more minutes until snack time. My flashlight of attention notices some gurgling in my stomach. I am getting hungry! Let me take a deep breath and shift my flashlight back to my job for just a few more minutes."

T: "I know that standardized tests are stressful. Before we begin, let's sit quietly for a moment and check in with our bodies. Notice your shoulders. Are they raised? Notice your jaw. Is it clenched? Take a deep breath. You got this!"

T: "Waiting in line at lunch can be hard! Stop for a moment and feel your feet on the ground. Wiggle your toes in your shoes. Squeeze your hands into fists then relax them."

Plan for Success

How and when might you implement this concept? What spaces in the day might you use? Who might you call on for support/ideas? How might you handle potential roadblocks?

_____
_____
_____

Post-Teaching Reflection

What would you add or change? What worked and what didn't? What did your attention notice?

_____
_____
_____

Lesson, Differentiation, Modifications, and Notes

Trauma-Informed: Students with a history of trauma may experience discomfort placing their attention in their bodies. Always offer the breath or soles of the feet as an anchor, and keep participation in the body scan voluntary.

Neurodivergent: Consider physical challenges students may have when asked to engage in physical activity. Giving multiple options may be helpful (i.e., jogging in place or boxing punches). Students who struggle with self-regulation may benefit from close teacher proximity during the hook (e.g., jogging alongside the teacher, modeling the jumping jacks in front of the room) to avoid becoming dysregulated or overly silly.

English Learners: It may be helpful to point to body parts as you name them to reinforce the vocabulary for ELs.

Gifted Learners: Prior to the lesson, ask students to research the term *interoception* and share what they learned. Ask students to summarize the concepts in the lesson or reteach those who may have missed the lesson or need a refresher.

Notes:

★ It may be helpful to briskly review what was learned in previous microlessons before beginning this one.

★ You might use terms like cardiovascular system, sympathetic and parasympathetic nervous system, resting heart rate, etc. with older students. If you do incorporate, be sure to keep the focus on the shifting of attention and the noticings.

Sample Early Elementary Body Scan Script

Right, now we are going to practice moving our attention throughout our bodies starting at the top of our heads and moving all the way to our toes. Practicing moving our attention helps us get better at focusing, and can help us relax and be ready to learn!

Bring your flashlight of attention to the top of your head. Squeeze all the muscles in your face nice and tight. Squeeze, squeeze, squeeze … aaaand release!

Bring your flashlight of attention to your shoulders. Squeeze all the muscles in your shoulders and arms. Squeeze, squeeze, squeeze … aaaand release!

Continue down the body, squeezing and releasing. Ask students what they notice about their bodies and minds after completing the body scan. Optional: Each student may fill in the Thoughts-Emotions-Sensations practice sheet with their noticings.

Sample Middle Elementary Body Scan Script

Right now we are going to practice moving our attention throughout our bodies starting at the top of our heads and moving all the way to our toes. Practicing moving our attention helps us get better at focusing, and can help us relax and be ready to learn!

Sit up tall in your chair with your arms by your sides. Begin to turn your eyes and ears inward to listen to the body and pay attention to how you are feeling. Breathe slowly in and out. Repeat. In and out. Excellent work. Bring your attention to your toes on your left foot. How do they feel? Now check your left ankle. Can you feel it? If not, wiggle it a little bit. Now check in with your left leg. Is there any stress or tension there? Take a deep breath. Imagine that you are releasing any tension that you find, like pulling the lid off a jar of steam. Good! Let's focus on the toes of your right foot. Wiggle them a bit. How do they feel? Let go of any tension that you find. Now your right ankle. Now pay attention to your right leg. Breathe. Relax. Excellent! Now we check in with your lower back. How is your back touching the floor or chair? How does your stomach feel? Any time you find some stress, just let it go, like a puff of steam into the air. Good. Pay attention to the back of your neck. How does it feel? Check in with your head. Does it feel light or heavy? Feel your ears, the roots of your hair, your forehead, your cheeks. Can you feel your teeth? How do they feel? How does your tongue feel inside your mouth? Feel the top of your head. Breathe. Relax. Did you find tension anywhere? If so, just allow it to melt into the floor, to fall away from you. Now sit quietly for a few seconds. Check out your whole body. Imagine a cloud of relaxation is ready to swish right over all of you, taking with it any stress or tension that you found. Great work! Now you know just where stress or tension likes to hide in your body.

Sample Middle and High School Body Scan Script

Right now we are going to complete a body scan. We will move our attention through the body to notice what's happening in each part. If you get distracted or your mind wanders away from the exercise, that is okay and very normal. Be patient with yourself and simply bring your attention back to the exercise without judging yourself.

1. Sit in a comfortable position in your chair. You can also do this exercise lying down in a comfortable position on your back with your legs and arms outstretched.

2. If you are lying down for this exercise, you can close your eyes; however, if you notice you start to drift off or fall asleep, open your eyes into a relaxed gaze to remain awake.

3. Rest your hands comfortably on your lap or by your side if you are lying down.

4. Now let's start by taking a few deep breaths. As you exhale, notice your body. Simply observe your natural breath for a few moments. Inhaling and exhaling in your own time.

5. Let's move now to focus on your feet. Simply bring your attention to your feet. You may notice some tingling or the ground under your feet; your shoes or your clothing touching your feet. Pressure, tightness, looseness. Simply notice the sensations. Notice your toes, the arch of your feet, the tops and sides of your feet. Scan and observe them, noticing any sensations that are present. Avoid labeling, judging, liking or disking the things you notice. Just allow yourself to observe the sensations present around your feet.

6. If at any time during this body scan your mind wanders, just notice what it's doing. Perhaps you notice it "thinking, thinking," "remembering, remembering," or "planning, planning" ... just notice what it's doing silently. And bring your attention back to your breath and the part of the body you are paying attention to.

7. Now move your attention to your ankles, shins and your calves. Notice any sensations that might be present there. If you notice any tightness in your muscles here, let go of that resistance and tightness and simply notice the sensations present in that area. You may notice your clothing, or the air, or even pain. Notice anything you find as a sensation. Even with pain, avoid liking, disliking or rejecting it – just allow yourself to notice it as a sensation in your body.

8. Now move your attention to your knees and the backs of your knees. Pay attention to any sensations around there. What do you notice? Again, avoid judging what you notice, and just kindly observe your knees and the sensations in that area.

9. Gently shift your attention now to your thighs. The back and front of your thighs. What do you notice there? Maybe your clothing or tingling? The temperature in your skin? You might notice the sensation of your thigh muscles, or the areas where they touch your chair, and where they don't touch your chair. Simply notice your thighs. If you notice tension in this area or in any area as we move through this Body Scan, play with letting it go as you observe.

10. Remember if your mind wanders, just notice what it's doing. Then come back to focusing on your breath and the part of the body you are looking at.

11. Let's move to your sit-bones, your seat, and your pelvic area. Once again you may notice sensations like tension, temperature, or clothing as you observe this area. Remember, as you notice sensations, avoid labeling, judging, liking or disliking them. If your mind is judging, thinking, or wandering, simply bring your attention back to your breath and continue to observe this area of your body.

12. Now move your attention to your lower abdomen and lower back. Scanning these areas for sensations. Make sure your abdominal muscles are relaxed and soft, as it allows you to breathe more deeply and easily. Notice any sensations present here, breathing naturally.

13. Expand your awareness to include your upper abdomen and middle back. What do you notice here? Some people hold stress or anxiety in their abdomen. Don't resist any sensations, just notice them. Notice the life in your body, as it communicates to you what's going on, through these sensations. Allow yourself to be with the sensations, making sure your breath is flowing, naturally and comfortably.

14. Let's focus next on your chest and upper back. Notice whatever sensations are there. Allow them just to be present. Making sure you do not judge, like, dislike, or reject. Simply notice. Many people hold tension in the chest, upper back and shoulders. If that's the case for you, just notice the tension as a sensation, and play with letting it go.

15. Again, if your mind wanders, notice what it's doing. Notice the thoughts passing by, and gently bring your attention back to your breath and the part of your body you are focusing on.

16. Now, shifting your attention to your shoulders. Notice the sensations there, whatever they might be. You might notice temperature, your clothing, the air, any tension present there. Allow yourself to notice these as sensations. Are you tightening your shoulders? If so, allow them to relax, and continue to scan your shoulders, noticing anything that comes up.

17. Now move your attention to your arms. Begin scanning from your shoulders down to your elbows and then down to your wrists, hands and fingers. Notice any sensations present for you. You may notice your arms touching the rest of your body, your temperature, or your clothing, or the air around them. You may notice your muscles. If you notice tension in your muscles, simply let go of the tension and continue to observe these areas of your body.

18. Now move your attention to your neck. Scan the front and back of your neck. Observe the sides of your neck, noticing whatever is there. Is there tightness, tingling, hair touching your skin? Whatever is there, just notice it. Notice the inside of your neck. Remember, avoid judging, liking or disliking what you notice. Simply observe this part of your body, and play with letting go of any tension you might notice. Breathing and relaxing as you notice this part of your body.

19. Shift your attention next to your head – the back of your head, sides of your head, and top of your head. Simply notice whatever sensations you notice there. Notice your forehead, your temples, your jaw. If you notice any tension or tightness, simply let it go. If there is any pain or discomfort, notice it as a sensation.

20. Some of these sensations are very subtle, so you really need to focus your attention on them. Continue to scan down your face, your eyes, cheek bones, your ears, your hair, chin. Pay attention to the sensations you notice. Whatever is there, just notice it, kindly observing without judgment, breathing naturally.

21. And finally notice the sensations in your whole body, at once. Allow yourself to feel your whole body, and the sensations in it, all at the same time. When you are ready, you can bring that to a close. Gently open your eyes to complete the body scan.

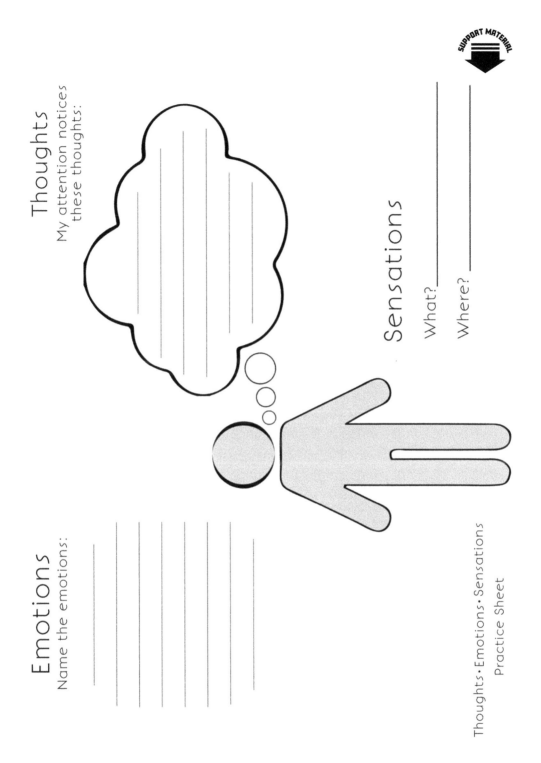

Thoughts

My attention notices these thoughts:

Emotions

Name the emotions:

Sensations

What?

Where?

Thoughts·Emotions·Sensations
Practice Sheet

References

CMIND (2021). *The tree of contemplative practices [illustration].* The Center for Contemplative Mind in Society. https://www.contemplativemind.org/practices/tree.

Jennings, P. A. (2020). *Teacher burnout turnaround.* W.W. Norton & Company.

Santoro, D. (2018). *Demoralized.* Harvard Education Press.

5

The Lie

I'm Stressed Because I'm Constantly Being Asked to Do More, with Less

The Truth: Stress is unavoidable; how we respond dictates our levels of suffering and discomfort.

 Key Concepts in This Chapter:

★ Stress is a universal human experience.
★ Stress can lead to unwanted behaviors and habits.
★ Chronic stress leads to burnout and other health problems.
★ Completing the stress cycle helps return the body and brain to equilibrium.

I pull my car into the school pick-up line as a mom friend texts me:

Her: Is that you behind me?
Me: Yes! Hiiiii
Her: Hiiiii wanna hit the park? Haven't seen you in so long!
Me: I know! Ugh sorry I can't today. I have to rush home to get Talula to gymnastics then throw dinner together while taking a conference call. Maybe … next week?

This situation repeats weekly.

DOI: 10.4324/9781003316275-5

Good Morning; Let the Stress Begin!

I recently read a meme that said "Adult friendships are texting back and forth to make plans then reschedule plans until you die." The one thing people agree upon is that everyone is so very busy; especially teachers. Their busy-ness becomes their badge of honor, and they feel a real sense of pride when items get crossed off their lengthy to-do lists. It feels natural to most people to frantically scurry around all day to the point of collapse. What would happen if people paused for a moment and thought – is this really living? In her book, The *Top 5 Regrets of the Dying* (2011), Bronnie Ware, a palliative care nurse outlines five themes from caring for patients during their final days. Two of the regrets outlined by Ware are: 1. I wish I hadn't worked so hard, and 2. I wish I had let myself be happier. Many people are working themselves to the bone, only pausing to reflect when faced with illness or death.

There are countless books, articles, podcasts, organizations, pills, vitamins, and therapies designed to help children and adults reduce and manage stress. In fact, the global stress management treatment market is expected to reach $20.6 billion by 2024 (www.bccresearch.com).

> **Human beings are spending billions of dollars attempting to solve a self-made problem.**

"Emotional stress is a major contributing factor to the six leading causes of death in the United States: cancer, coronary heart disease, accidental injuries, respiratory disorders, cirrhosis of the liver and suicide" (Salleh, 2008). Human beings were not designed to work 14-hour days while caring for small children, aging parents, and managing a household – yet this is the current reality. When "frustrated, overworked, or disrespected teachers offer little patience or kindness in their interactions with students," (Milkie & Warner, 2011) teacher stress is inadvertently absorbed by students. Teachers can learn to put stress in its place as a useful biological tool rather than a silent killer that leads to disease and death.

Stress – Are We Addicted?

For years I have watched teachers' jaws drop in horror when I ask them to mentally put down their to-do lists for five to seven minutes per day. There is a palpable fear that if they put down their stress, they will drop the ball. The other day I started thinking about all of the balls teachers keep in the air on a daily basis. It made me wonder: how did teachers end up solely responsible for all of these balls? What happens when teachers put them down?

Do Teachers Even *Enjoy* Juggling?

As a novice teacher I scoffed at the idea of pausing to breathe or (God forbid) take an actual break because I was afraid that if I shifted my focus off work, I would not get everything done. My mind felt scattered - and oddly addicted to this way of operating. As I taught a reading group, in my mind I was rehearsing the writing lesson I needed to teach next. I had to operate in overdrive, because I believed that if I slowed down just for a moment, I might completely shut down or somehow not be able to efficiently carry out my daily tasks. Living in a state of heightened stress and time urgency shortened my patience with my students and often rendered my days joyless. Teacher stress is linked with burnout and absenteeism (Ryan et al.,

2017) and is one of the predictors of teacher attrition (Harmsen et al., 2018;

Ryan et al., 2017). How can teachers possibly perform at their best if they are chronically stressed?

Pause and Reflect

How often do you find yourself teaching in overdrive? What are your fear-based beliefs around dropping the ball?

_____

_____

_____

When Teachers Misbehave

Teachers act as emotional leaders for their students. "In this role, intentionally managing our stress and emotions can make a huge difference in our students' engagement, motivation and prosocial behavior." (Jennings, 2020). Chronic stress shapes the way teachers think, relate to colleagues, and teach students. Teachers lacking social and emotional competence unknowingly fan the flames of misbehavior, and may even misbehave themselves. There are a few key moments I remember from my own early elementary years – the second-grade talent show where I danced to Kokomo, the fifth-grade trip to the Jersey shore, and two times I was scolded by my teachers. I will never forget my fourth-grade teacher telling me that if I "weren't so focused on boys I would have done better on my spelling test," and I certainly will always remember my sixth-grade teacher telling my friend and I that he gave us some rope and we were "hanging ourselves with it." When teaching in survival mode, teachers cannot access patience, problem solving skills, and compassion. Do I think these comments made them bad teachers? No. Frustrated, overworked, and underpaid? Absolutely.

A Closer Look at Stress

In mindfulness practice we are trained to look at stress with a nonjudgmental and curious awareness, which is what we will practice now.

✍ **Pause and Reflect**

List your personal and professional stressors. Be specific. For example, what about "work" is stressful?

_____

_____

_____

Next, think about the effects stress has on your mind and body. Where in your body do you feel stress? What does it feel like? How does stress affect the way you eat, sleep, and behave?

_____

_____

_____

Last, write a simple one sentence definition for stress.

_____

_____

_____

Below is a summary of the most common teacher responses informally collected over ten+ years.

Many teachers easily list stressors and their effects, but struggle to define stress. Some definitions include:

♦ Stress is a feeling you get when you are overwhelmed.
♦ Stress is when there are too many things to do and not enough time to do them.
♦ Stress is an emotion that makes it hard to concentrate.

Stress is complex and definitions of stress vary across scientific fields. Whereas the medical field defines stress in a biological context, the psychological definition includes the mental perception of the event and the body's response to

Table 5.1 Common Stressors and Effects

Stressors	Effects
Finances (bills, loan payments)	Lack of sleep
Health (my own, my children's, parents)	Eating more/less
Lack of time to do everything	Frustration, Anger
Administration demands	Stomach/headaches
Student misbehavior	No motivation

it. Building a broad understanding of the basic physiology of stress empowers teachers to appropriately course correct rather than continue to suffer.

Stress in the Brain and Body

Although each teacher experiences stress differently, the events inside the body and brain remain the same. First, *your brain perceives a threat*. The amygdala, an almond-shaped structure in your midbrain, sends a distress signal to your hypothalamus. Long ago when humans lived in caves, diligently avoiding threats was essential to remaining alive. Many threats loomed outside the cave like armed cave people ready to attack and saber-toothed tigers on the prowl for food. Threats were imminent and deadly. Take a look back at the stressors you listed. These are the *threats* of modern society – many of them *psychological* rather than *physical*. Even though paying bills is not life threatening, the human brain perceives this threat the same way it would a hungry tiger looking for a human snack.

> **Your brain doesn't speak the language of "too many meetings," it only understands "threat," and reacts accordingly.**

The threat might be real or imagined. For example, a teacher might be physically sitting in a challenging meeting with a supervisor, or *thinking* about the meeting – beforehand, in anticipation of it going badly or afterward, in regret of how it was handled.

Next, the **sympathetic nervous system** enacts the fight, flight, freeze response. Once the **hypothalamus** receives the message that there is a threat (real or perceived) from the **amygdala**, it begins communicating with other glands to begin readying the body to ward off the threat. The pituitary gland tells the adrenal glands, which sit above the kidneys, to make and secrete adrenaline and cortisol. **Epinephrine** pushes blood to the arms and legs, increases heart rate, dilates the lungs, and sharpens the senses. **Glucose** is released into cells for added energy. **Cortisol** signals the body to circulate substances to help repair cells and tissue – just in case that tiger chomps down on a limb. Meanwhile, **endorphins** help the brain ignore pain signals. Digestive and reproductive systems are suppressed, because the body prioritizes self-preservation over all else. Human bodies react in some variation of fighting off the threat, fleeing or running, or playing dead. Teachers obviously cannot punch their supervisors or run out of the classroom into the street, yet the fight, flight, or freeze response still needs to be carried out in some capacity. But, have no fear, because humans have evolved into fancy modern ways of fighting, running, and freezing. There are two additional threat responses, often discussed in psychology as trauma responses, which include "fawning" – people pleasing, and "flopping" – becoming apathetic and depressed.

Table 5.2 Modernizing Fight/Flight/Freeze

Threat Response	What It Looked like in the Past	What It Looks like Today
Fight	physically attack the animal/other human	yelling; arguing; snapping at others
Flight	run away	avoiding or self-distracting with technology; food; alcohol; etc.
Freeze	play dead; immobilize	staying in bed; refusing to engage

Stress is unavoidable and in appropriate amounts, can serve as a motivator. However, most teachers, nurses, and those in helping professions experience prolonged periods of intense stress, creating cortisol imbalance. An ongoing drip of adrenaline and cortisol into the bloodstream results in lowered immunity, higher inflammation, weight gain, and disease. Dysregulated cortisol levels contribute to anxiety, depression, digestive problems, headaches, muscle tension and pain, heart disease, heart attack, high blood pressure and stroke, sleep problems, weight gain, and memory and concentration impairment.

When the stress response is switched on, the brain and body enter survival mode. Systems in the brain and body are all thrown out of whack, which means outside of tracking the threat, most of our precious foundational skills go offline.

Completing the Stress Cycle

> **Just because you've dealt with the stressor doesn't mean you've dealt with the stress itself.**
>
> Nagoski & Nagoski, 2020

I had a dog that would dart to the window barking like crazy every time the mailman approached the front door. Afterward he would trot away, proud of himself for saving my life, and shake his body out as if I had just brought him in from the rain. Dogs intuitively *shake off* to help their bodies metabolize chemicals after threatening events, thus completing the stress cycle. Humans are not as fortunate. Stress hormones continually wreak havoc in the bloodstream, because humans oftentimes do not complete the stress cycle. All other mammals twitch, shudder, and shake after life-threatening events. Running from a tiger burns off adrenaline, shuts down the stress response, and completes the stress cycle which brings us back to a calm, abiding state of homeostasis. It is the physical exertion of running or fighting that completes the stress cycle and calms the brain and body. Teachers can find ways to complete the many stress cycles that begin throughout the day by getting enough physical exercise, practicing mindful breathing, laughing, or giving/receiving loving affection. In their book, *Burnout: The Secret to Unlocking the Stress Cycle*, Nagoski and Nagoski (2020) introduce a practice called the 20-second hug. When mammals embrace for at least 20 seconds, oxytocin, or the cuddle hormone as it's often called, is released to counterbalance and diffuse stress chemicals. Whether it be a warm embrace, a quick game of freeze dance with your students, or a good belly laugh – these completion exercises are essential to bringing our much-needed foundational skills back online.

Teacher Lesson

Notice, Pause, Name

The key to managing stress is to (ironically) step closer to it, as if examining the stress under a microscope. Adopting a mindful and curious attitude toward our own bodies and minds provide insights into how our thoughts, emotions, and sensations interact during the stress response.

Notice, Pause, Name
For the next few weeks, try to notice when you are *beginning* to feel stressed. Is your jaw clenched tightly? Are your shoulders hiked all the way to your ears? Maybe you are breathing shallowly into your chest, or you feel a throb behind your eyes. Simply **notice** these first signs of stress. Then, **pause**. Take a few deep breaths in and out of the nostrils, staying aware of the sensations in your body. Mentally note the stress, silently saying, "This is the stress response," followed by "I am safe in this moment right now." **Naming** the stress response allows you to activate your prefrontal cortex, bringing your foundational skills back online and activating your parasympathetic rest and digest system.

Tips for Success

- ◆ Human brains are motivated by curiosity, therefore treat this as a self-experiment and try to remain curious, even in times of stress.
- ◆ Language matters – objectively name the stress response by mentally noting, "Ah, this is the stress response," rather than "I'm so stressed." Do not "I" and "my" stress.
- ◆ Thoughts can ignite and perpetuate the stress response. Try using the Thoughts-Emotions-Sensations Practice Sheet in Chapter 4 to parse apart these three areas of your experience in times of stress.

3:5 Breath Practice

Simply noticing your stress is a great start to calming the brain and body. Here is another practice to try. The 3:5 Breath Practice is a quick and portable way to complete your stress cycles. Try it, now. Rate your current stress level on a scale of 1–5, 1 representing minimal stress and 5 representing extreme stress: Record it here: ___ Next, set a timer to practice two minutes of 3:5 Breathing, lengthening the inhale to the count of 3, and the exhale to the count of 5. You may incorporate physical movement by raising straight arms to shoulder height as you inhale, and lowering the arms to your sides as you exhale.

Now, re-rate your stress level: _____ What does your attention notice?

This week, choose a few stress cycle completion exercises to incorporate into your school day. Practice pausing, noticing, and naming your stress response. Modeling prosocial ways to manage stress helps students regulate their behaviors and engage fully in their learning.

> **Pause and Reflect**
> What did your attention notice after spending a week or more completing your stress cycles and pausing, noticing, and naming your stress response?

Remember that the goal of mindfulness is not to *get rid of* stress. Rather than avoiding, the suggestion is to embrace stress with kindness and curiosity. For many people this is a new way of relating to stress, and therefore takes patience and practice to build new neural connections and form a habit.

Five-Minute Student Microlesson

Stress Response

This microlesson was designed for students aged 7–12. See notes for younger and older students.

Concepts

Stress is a natural and normal human experience. Too much stress can make it hard to learn and remember information.

Why it matters: When you notice your stress, you can take action to calm down your brain so it can think and perform at its best.

Delivery

Hook: Anecdote: Teacher tells a genuine story about stress getting in the way of concentration. Be sure to explicitly state how attention noticed sensations in the body (e.g., tension, tightness) and difficult thoughts. Example: T: "Over the weekend I was reading a news article and when I came to the last sentence I realized that I had no idea what I had read! My mind was full of worrisome thoughts about a big meeting I had with our principal. My shoulders felt tight and my belly was clenched. I was so stressed that I couldn't concentrate or remember what I was reading."

T: "Thumbs up if you have ever felt worried or stressed before. Turn and talk to share an example with a partner." Ask for a student or two to share aloud. Be sure to reinforce the concept that a stressed brain cannot learn and remember information.

Demonstrate: T: "I often pause while doing my work and use my flashlight of attention to notice stressful thoughts or tension in my body. When I notice stress, I can choose to take action, like practice 3:5 Breathing. Watch me demonstrate this, now." Teacher demonstrates 3:5 Breathing.

Participate: T: "Let's try a few rounds of 3:5 Breathing together. I will count as you breathe."

Thread: T: "Before a test, or after we finish a big assignment we might pause and notice if our brains and bodies feel stressed. We can use 3:5 Breathing to help us manage our stress and return to feeling calm and ready to learn."

Model: *(examples)*

T: "We are beginning a new writing assignment, and sometimes writing can be challenging. My flashlight is noticing thoughts like, *Ugh! I don't like writing.* My jaw feels tight. I'm going to try some 3:5 Breathing before we begin."

T: "It's time to transition our desks to testing positions. We move the desks to prepare the room for the state test. We can practice 3:5 Breathing to prepare our brains. Try 3 rounds on your own once your desk is in position."

Plan for Success

How and when might you implement this concept? What spaces in the day might you use? Who might you call on for support/ideas? How might you handle potential roadblocks?

_____

_____

_____

Post-Teaching Reflection

What would you add or change? What worked and what didn't? What did your attention notice?

_____

_____

_____

 Lesson Differentiation, Modification, and Notes

Trauma-Informed: Students with anxiety may feel triggered by breath practices. Always present these practices as optional. You can also provide alternate places to rest the attention like the soles of the feet or the sounds in the room.

Neurodivergent: See *Trauma-Informed* notes above.

English Learners: When introducing a complex concept like stress, it is important to first provide information in a student's native language. Also note that cultures and families vary on how openly emotions are modeled and discussed which may influence the turn and talk.

Gifted Learners: Ask students to investigate the hand model of the brain by Daniel Siegel, and report back to the class on how we "flip our lid" in times of stress.

Notes:

★ Middle and upper grades may benefit from the teacher sharing a diagram of the brain, indicating how in times of stress, MRI's show amygdala area activation with decreased activity in the Prefrontal Cortex (PFC), where the brain executes foundational skills.

★ Younger students (5–7) may not be as familiar with the word *stress* and may need some additional language like *worried, nervous*, etc. during the Hook.

★ Be sure to normalize feeling stressed, noting how sometimes stress can cause stomach upset, sleep disturbances, changes in eating patterns, etc.
★ Be prepared with resources for students who many overshare about their stress levels (e.g., on-campus guidance counselors or social workers).

References

Harmsen, R., Helms-Lorenz, M., Maulana, R., & van Veen, K. (2018). The relationship between beginning teachers' stress causes, stress responses, teaching behaviour and attrition. *Teachers and Teaching*, 24(6), 626–643. DOI: 10.1080/13540602.2018.14654041.

Jennings, P. A. (2020). *Teacher burnout turnaround*. W.W. Norton & Company.

Milkie, M. A., & Warner, C. H. (2011). Classroom learning environments and the mental health of first grade children. *Journal of Health and Social Behavior*, 52(1), 4–22. https://doi.org/10.1177/0022146510394952.

Nagoski, E., & Nagoski, A. (2020). *Burnout: The secret to unlocking the stress cycle*. Random House Publishing Group.

Salleh, M. R. (2008). Life event, stress and illness. *The Malaysian Journal of Medical Sciences*, 15(4), 9–18.

Ryan, S. V., von der Embse, N. P., Pendergast, L. L., Saeki, E., Segool, N., & Schwing, S. (2017). Leaving the teaching profession: The role of teacher stress and educational accountability policies on turnover intent. *Teaching and Teacher Education*, 66, 1–11. https://doi.org/10.1016/j.tate.2017.03.016.

Ware, B. (2011). *Top 5 regrets of the dying*. Hay House, Inc.

6

The Lie

I Can't Help Feeling Overwhelmed All of the Time

The Truth: Strengthening foundational skills empowers teachers to manage strong emotions and reduce overwhelm.

 Key Concepts in This Chapter:
★ Emotions are transient, and often carry a message.
★ Strong emotions can cause unwanted behaviors.
★ Mindfulness practices help teachers return to homeostasis.

An overwhelmed teacher snaps at a student. An exhausted supervisor replies to a parent email with a snarky comment. An annoyed administrator raises his voice in a staff meeting. Overwhelm. Exhaustion. Annoyance.

Human beings experience a vast range of emotions, some pleasant and others less so. Difficult emotions are often blamed for antisocial behaviors, because the space between the experience of an emotion and acting on it is very hard to find. Although there are many ways to define it, "an emotion is a complex psychological state that involves three distinct components: a subjective experience, a physiological response, and a behavioral or expressive response" (Hockenbury & Hockenbury, 2007). For example, an excited student en route to a field trip may smile or clap – the expressive response, and experience an increased heart rate – the physiological response. The emotion

DOI: 10.4324/9781003316275-6

of excitement is individual to the student. It is subjective, meaning that other students may not feel the same way. Strong foundational skills allow students and teachers to shift into objectively noticing and naming emotions as they occur. Slowing down, inhabiting the present moment, and clearly seeing emotions allows students to find the space to pause and respond with awareness, rather than react on autopilot.

A Typical Morning

As I pulled up to my school building at 6:50 am I thought about the exchange I had with my husband. I remembered rushing out of the kitchen with a travel mug of lukewarm coffee in hand. I noticed thoughts, like "He just doesn't seem to understand how much I do around the house! Would it kill him to fold and put away some laundry now and again?" I grabbed my belongings from the back seat of my Toyota, tote bags overflowing with papers, and headed into my classroom. As I passed by the office, I saw my colleague Yasmeen and a few other members of my grade-level team standing around the copier talking in a hushed whisper. Curious, I stopped to chat and learned that several teachers received upsetting emails from the administration that morning. Three veteran educators were being moved to different grades, with one teacher being moved to an *entirely different campus*. My stomach immediately dropped. I again noticed thoughts, only this time, they were a little more intense. "How can they do this? These teachers work so hard and have spent years perfecting their craft! Am I next?" My head spun as I entered my classroom, late, in a fog of stress.

My students streamed in behind me. I didn't get a chance to post the morning message or ready my materials for the day. I managed to trudge through first period, opened my email, and read that there was a mandatory staff meeting at 3:10pm which conflicted with an IEP meeting I had to run. Meanwhile, my husband texted me "Sorry about this morning. Can you grab the dry cleaning on the way home?" It wasn't yet noon and I was entirely overwhelmed. I thought, "I just cannot deal with today."

✒ Pause and Reflect

What thoughts do you notice after reading through the Typical Morning scenario? What do you sense in your body? How do you feel?

_____

_____

_____

Reflections from teachers:

> *"Wow. Just reading that made me stressed!"*
> *"I noticed my throat tightened up and I was holding my breath."*
> *"This sounds all too familiar. I found myself nodding my head as I read that scenario."*

As a young teacher, I bought into this lie that **to be a teacher meant to be overwhelmed most of the time**. This myth matched my experience – most days I was surviving rather than thriving. It seemed that most of my colleagues were also overwhelmed, which validated and further cemented this lie into my brain. My mood and behavior reflected this state of overwhelm, negatively impacting my teaching and my students' learning.

Understanding Human Emotions

Dr. Richard Davidson, founder of the Center for Healthy Minds at the University of Wisconsin at Madison, is at the forefront of research on affective neuroscience. His research investigates how mindfulness affects emotions. In his New York Times bestseller, *The Emotional Life of Your Brain* (2013) Dr. Davidson explains the difference between emotional states, traits, moods, and styles. An emotional *state* is fleeting, while a feeling that spans minutes or hours or even days is a *mood*. An emotional *style* describes how a person generally feels, and develops over years.

Referring to my Typical Morning scenario, I experienced an emotional *state* of shock and fear after I heard the news of the staff reshuffling. Having an emotional *style* that errs on the side of less resilient, this negatively affected my *mood* for the day. In contrast, my colleague Yasmeen's emotional style was characterized by positivity and greater resiliency. At baseline, she was calm and relaxed, and tended to allow stress to roll off her back. When I passed her in the hallway after lunch, she smiled and carried on like nothing happened. She was clearly able to handle the upset better than I, and did not allow the news to negatively impact her mood.

📝 **Pause and Reflect**

Are you inherently resilient, bouncing back like Yasmeen or are you more emotionally rigid like myself? To learn more about your emotional style, visit https://centerhealthyminds.org/join-the-movement/whats-your-emotional-style to see where you stand against the six dimensions of resilience, outlook, social intuition, self-awareness, sensitivity to context, and attention.

Overwhelm – What Is It?

Although not enjoyable, overwhelm is a normal human emotion. It is experienced when the demands of the situation are greater than the resources at hand. In the Typical Morning scenario, I began the day preoccupied and stressed about an exchange I had with my husband. Hearing the news about the teacher reshuffle added to my already stressed nervous system. Beginning my lesson unprepared then reading the email and text that followed put the demands of the day above my threshold of resources to process and manage them. My internal resources (i.e., my sense of calm and groundedness, levels of dopamine and serotonin) were not able to metabolize the mounting stress chemicals efficiently enough

to remain calm and clear-headed. Once the scales were tipped and my stress response was firing, my thoughts fed the blaze and kept it roaring hot.

What would have happened if I paused for a moment before entering the building to take a breath, calm my body and mind, and let go of the exchange

I had in the kitchen? How would the day have unfolded if I asked Yasmeen to cover my class for five minutes so I could run to the bathroom or step outside to reset before beginning first period? How would that have changed my emotional state, and my day as a whole?

Pause and Reflect

How often do you feel overwhelmed? To what degree does overwhelm influence your mood?

_____

_____

_____

Overwhelm and Burnout

Although human emotions are universal, the severity to which we experience emotions differs from person to person. Overwhelm registers throughout my entire body. My body feels numb and sometimes paralyzed, while my thoughts race. My mind tells me to do more and do it faster while my body feels trapped in quicksand. I know that when I'm experiencing overwhelm, I need to be on the lookout for its cousins: cynicism and a sense of underperformance. Together, these three pieces make up work-place burnout.

Overwhelm + Cynicism + Sense of Unaccomplishment = Workplace Burnout

It is important for teachers to notice and name their emotions, especially the ones that feel challenging. Emotions often have a message. Fear says _this is not safe_ while joy says _this is amazing, let's have more of this!_ When teachers train themselves to pause and tune in to their bodies and minds, they can allow emotions to pass through their experience and return to equilibrium. It is in this state of calm homeostasis that the magic of effective teaching and learning can occur.

Emotions – How Many?

Many factors affect personal distress tolerance, including one's lived experiences, family histories of trauma, daily stress levels, and foundational skill sets. One teacher may easily tolerate increased demands at work while another teacher responds with an emotional breakdown in the parking lot after school. A novice teacher may find herself experiencing overwhelm daily or weekly until she becomes more comfortable with her job. When I'm leading a professional development workshop I often ask teachers to write a list of emotions. The longest list usually contains about 20 emotions, when there are actually 34,000 distinguishable feelings (Goleman, 2004). These feelings are in a constant state of flux, sometimes changing moment by moment as the events of the classroom unfold. Without a strong anchor to the present moment, teachers can feel like an emotional pinball getting knocked around.

Some emotions are difficult to experience. Simply put, they just don't feel pleasant. It is normal to push away fear and anger and welcome joy and contentment. However, what we resist, persists – avoidance behaviors like eating, scrolling, or shopping delay the processing of emotion, prolonging the suffering.

Emotions as Visitors

Mindfulness taught me to notice the moments of my life with a kind, curious stance. When I was in college I struggled with depression, especially in the gray winter months in the northeast. By February I couldn't get out of bed, eat healthy foods, and keep up with an exercise routine. I thought, "I'm depressed," as if the depression was *me* or *mine* or who I *was*. One particularly long winter, a friend introduced me to Tara Brach, a best-selling author, psychologist and meditation teacher. I began reading books and listening to online teachings by Jon Kabat-Zinn and Thich Nhat Hanh. I started to experience my emotions in a different way. Mindfulness practice teaches that emotions are impermanent and impersonal.

Emotions are visitors stopping by, asking for attention, recognition, and acceptance. When teachers "roll out the welcome mat" (Kabat-Zinn, 2020) for both positive and negative emotions by recognizing the actuality of what is, they adopt an attitude of awareness and compassion to *all* emotions. Reframing my feelings of depression as emotional visitors, temporarily hanging out in my body and mind for a finite period of time, allowed me to feel less overwhelmed. Although a subtle shift, this **cognitive reappraisal** is very helpful during emotional storms.

Although I didn't know it at the time, I was building my foundational skills. Slowly I began to practice managing my attention, regulating my emotions, and becoming more self-aware. I started walking into the classroom with more clarity, which allowed me to better serve my students.

Emotion Regulation

It is time to put emotions in their place. Like stress, turning toward powerful emotions rather than away is the most effective management strategy. Most teachers do not *want* to feel angry, sad or even overwhelmed. In fact, many teachers look at me like I have two heads when I encourage them to *turn toward* strong emotions. However, doing so with a calm, abiding presence cultivated through our mindfulness practice allows teachers to skillfully manage the waves of emotion without getting knocked down again and again.

Pause and Reflect

How do you usually react to challenging emotions?

_____

_____

_____

_____

_____

Teacher Lesson

R.A.I.N.

The R.A.I.N. practice is a tool to help regulate strong emotions. It allows for the creation of a container for emotion, allowing teachers to stay tethered to a calm, abiding presence during times of upset.

R.A.I.N.
Find a quiet place where you will be undisturbed for seven to ten minutes. Find a comfortable seated posture with your hands resting in your lap. Place your feet flat on the floor, allowing your spine to rise up out of your pelvis. Drop your shoulders down your back. Loosen your jaw and relax your brow. Make whatever adjustments you need to be one percent more comfortable. Call to mind a scenario from the day or week when you experienced a strong emotion (e.g., an email from a parent, a difficult student behavior, etc.). Visualize the experience. Replay the event in your mind, reliving the thoughts, emotions, and sensations in your body if you can.

R – Recognize. Identify and acknowledge what you feel. Silently name the emotion by saying, "This is [emotion]." Note that more than one emotion may be experienced simultaneously.

A – Accept. Inhale and exhale as you accept the emotion. You might silently say "This emotion is visiting right now, and that's okay." There is no use avoiding it, because what we resist, persists. Breathe in, and breathe out. Say hello to the emotion with a smile if you can manage it! Accept its presence, however uncomfortable.

I – Investigate. Draw your attention into your body. What physical sensations accompany this emotion? What is the level of intensity? Do not attempt to change anything – simply witness the physical sensations in your body right now. Now shift your attention to notice your thoughts. What thoughts are feeding the emotion? Observe the thoughts with kindness.

N – Non-identify and Nurture. Remind yourself that many humans across the globe are experiencing the same emotion that you are right at this moment. You are not alone in your moment of struggle. Hold yourself with compassion as you would a dear friend. This emotion is not you, it is simply a visitor that you can observe and allow to pass through.

Tips for Success

◆ It may be helpful to first practice R.A.I.N. with a positive emotion like excitement, anticipation, or joy before moving to a more challenging emotion like fear, anger, or jealousy.

◆ The more you practice R.A.I.N. in times of calm, the better you will be able to use it in times of unrest. Do not wait until you feel overwhelmed or extremely anxious to try the practice for the first time.

◆ When first learning the technique, avoid practicing with an extremely intense emotion like panic or rage.

Pause and Reflect

Try out the R.A.I.N. practice this week, then come back to reflect. What did your attention notice during the R.A.I.N. practice?

_____

_____

_____

Five-Minute Student Microlesson

Name It to Tame It
This microlesson is designed for students aged 10–16. See notes for younger students.

Concepts
Students learn that emotions are visitors seeking our attention. Naming challenging emotions helps "tame" them, allowing emotions to pass through efficiently.

Delivery
Hook: Teacher plays a song on repeat that evokes annoyance. For example, *The Song that Doesn't End* from Lamb Chop's Play Along, or *The Hampster Dance Song* by Hampton and the Hampsters. (These very annoying songs will work for any age group!) When students seem noticeably annoyed, stop the song. T: "Pause for a moment and notice how you're feeling after hearing that song multiple times. Turn and talk to share." Whip around the room allowing each student to briskly share one word describing how they feel. Repeats are okay!

Demonstrate: T: "Many of you felt annoyed or aggravated! Many of us don't enjoy feeling annoyed, mad, frustrated, bored, and many other strong emotions – but it's important to allow ourselves to feel them. Emotions come and go, and simply want our flashlights of attention. I'm going to put the song back on. This time, I will help you to notice how you feel and Name it to Tame it."

Participate: Teacher replays song then thinks aloud. T: "Ah, I'm noticing feeling annoyed. My chest feels heavy and my jaw is tight. It's okay, everybody feels this way, it will go away." Model taking a deep inhale and exhale. Encourage students to try talking to themselves in their head, noticing feeling annoyed/bored/mad, then naming the emotion.

Thread: T: "During the school day you will experience many emotions. Some might feel positive and enjoyable and others might not, and that's okay. Let's practice Name it to Tame it today when we are feeling frustrated."

Model: *(examples)*

T: "We are headed to lunch and recess. Many times we return to the classroom feeling annoyed about a disagreement we had outside. Practice using Name it to Tame it if you feel frustrated with one another."

T: "I can see you're upset. Let's sit down and take a deep breath. Notice your body. Notice your thoughts. Can you name the emotion that's here?"

Plan for Success

How and when might you implement this concept? What spaces in the day might you use? Who might you call on for support/ideas? How might you handle potential roadblocks?

_____

_____

_____

 Lesson Differentiation, Modifications, and Notes

Trauma-Informed: Shutting down emotions and dissociating is a common coping strategy for individuals who have endured physical, sexual, or emotional abuse. Understand that some students may have trouble accessing and naming any emotion at all, and that doing so may feel unsafe. Be sure to talk with your school guidance counselor or social worker before or after the lesson to share any specific concerns you may have.

Neurodivergent: Some students may have a lower threshold for annoyance than others. If you have a student prone to behavioral outbursts from annoyance or frustration, you may want to preview the lesson with the student or give the student a special job like controlling the music on your cue. Keep in mind that students diagnosed with Oppositional Defiant Disorder (ODD) may feel more comfortable and safe in states of anger, annoyance, and rage than they do in more vulnerable emotions like sadness, incompetence, or insecurity.

English Learners: Pre-teach emotional vocabulary (e.g., annoyed, aggravated) using pictures/photos of actual human faces. Use a translation tool (e.g., Google Translate) to help students access the content of the hook.

Gifted Learners: Note that academically gifted students may not also be socially or emotionally advanced. In fact, some students who favor logic, facts, and objectivity may struggle with SEL lessons and can benefit from some of the differentiation options presented here.

Notes:

★ All students may benefit from an emotion word bank in preparation for naming emotions. Younger students may be given four words like "happy, sad, silly, annoyed" with accompanying pictures while middle and older students may benefit from the Plutchik emotion wheel displayed on the smart board. (Simply google Plutchik emotion wheel or check here: https://positivepsychology.com/emotion-wheel/)

★ Younger students (K–2) or middle schoolers (6–8) may not find the Hook songs annoying. Instead, play a YouTube clip of a dog squeaky toy sound or an alarm clock sound – both very annoying!

★ Students (and adults) will confuse thoughts with emotions. For example, a student might say "I feel like I wanted the song to stop," to which you will prompt for an emotion word. These are teachable moments to help students learn to decipher thoughts from emotions.

References

Davidson, R., & Begley, S. (2013). *The emotional life of your brain*. Penguin.

Goleman, D. (2004). *Destructive emotions: A scientific dialogue with the Dalai Lama*. Bantam.

Hockenbury, D. H., & Hockenbury, S. E. (2007). *Discovering psychology* (4th ed.). Worth Publishers.

Kabat-Zinn, J. (2020, August 19). *Jon Kabat-Zinn Q & A: Putting out the welcome mat for both positive and negative feelings* [Video]. YouTube. www.youtube.com/watch?v=sGa_p1QQEfw.

7

The Lie

So and So (Insert Colleague/Boss/Student Name) Makes Me So Annoyed!

The Truth: Learning to respond to others with awareness vs. react on autopilot is a necessary skill for educators.

 Key Concepts in This Chapter:
★ Thoughts are not facts.
★ Beliefs can contribute to interpersonal conflicts.
★ Raising awareness of common thinking traps helps to avoid them.
★ All teachers experience triggers.
★ Responding with awareness to triggers reduces stress and improves compassion.

My Descent into Negativity

About two weeks prior to beginning my second year of teaching, I received an email informing me that I had a new position: co-teaching with a general education teacher. Mr. Brown, the general education teacher, was one of the few male teachers in the school and was well-liked by students and staff.

DOI: 10.4324/9781003316275-7

We were assigned the first full inclusion class in the district, which was both daunting and exciting. Historically, students with Individualized Education Plans (IEPs) received literacy and math instruction in the resource room – my glorified closet. The socialization and learning benefits of the inclusion model are strong, and I was eager to give my students what I truly felt was the least restrictive environment (LRE). When I arrived to set up my new classroom, I quickly realized that Mr. Brown had no idea that I would be in *his* classroom full time. Relatable, I know.

Needless to say, my co-teacher was not excited about my arrival, nor was he trained in the inclusion model. I will never forget the look on his face when the custodian dragged my huge desk through the classroom doorway. Mr. Brown wanted my desk in the back of the room, but I argued that my desk needed to be squeezed *next to* his in the *front* of the classroom so that I was perceived as an equal, not his *assistant*.

I cried in my car quite a bit that year. I felt defeated and oftentimes, offended. Mr. Brown and I struggled to find time to co-plan and disagreed about the pace of our teaching. I was disappointed by the segregation of *my* students, those with IEPs, from *his* students – the rest of the class. Dr. Jennifer Goeke (2020) discusses the challenges co-teaching pairs face. Teachers' varying expectations of students with disabilities, incongruent content knowledge, and general beliefs about co-teaching create tensions. These tensions smolder below the surface creating stress and aggravation which is easily transferred to students.

It was a challenging year fraught with disagreements, leaving me feeling like an intruder in what was supposed to be my own classroom. Looking back, I often wonder if there was something I could have done differently. Could I actually have *changed* my feelings?

Stinkin' Thinkin'

I believed that Mr. Brown was the problem, and blamed him for how I felt. I thought, "Mr. Brown is disrespectful. I cannot work with him. He should be better trained in co-teaching – then I would be happier. This entire year is going to be miserable. He is the reason why I am crying." Many times it was these thoughts, *not* what was actually happening, that led to my daily suffering and ultimately compromised how well I could do my job. The problem is that thoughts are not always true, and when left unexamined, thoughts drive behaviors.

> **Pause and Reflect**
>
> How can you relate to my co-teaching experience? What thoughts and emotions do your attention notice as you read the anecdote?
>
> _____
>
> _____
>
> _____
>
> _____
>
> _____

Cognitive Distortions

The attention system (orienting, alerting) notices three main domains of human experience: thoughts, emotions, and sensations in the body. The average person has over 6,000 thoughts per day. Many of these thoughts go unnoticed, while others captivate our attention. As the mind replays events of the past and worries about the future, it falls into thinking traps, or **cognitive distortions**. These distorted thoughts are untrue yet we believe them. Common cognitive distortions teachers experience are explained below.

Filtering: Magnifying the negative while filtering out the positive. A teacher may dwell on a single, unpleasant detail, resulting in a distorted recollection of the day. For example, a teacher thinks "My students were so talkative today," when in reality, *one* student would not stop talking.

Polarized/Black and White Thinking: Teachers sometimes believe that they must be perfect or they are a failure – there is no middle ground. This thinking style does not allow for shades of gray or allow for complexities of people or situations. Black and white thinking commonly involves words like *always* and *never*. For example, "I will *never* understand this new curriculum." "I *always* say the wrong thing."

Catastrophizing: Some teachers expect disaster to strike, with little to no evidence. They are inundated with *what ifs* and *worst-case-scenario* thoughts about the future. For example, "What if the meeting is a complete disaster," "What if my lesson flops?" "That child is going to be impossible to handle."

Shoulds: Teachers who fall into *the shoulds* have a list of ironclad rules against which they judge themselves and at times – others. They feel guilty or angry when the rules are violated. For example, a teacher may think,

"I really should stay late and redo that bulletin board. I shouldn't be so lazy," or "I should be better at conducting this new benchmark assessment by now." These thoughts lead to feelings of guilt and shame. When a person directs *should statements* toward others, the emotional consequences are often anger, frustration and resentment.

Pause and Reflect

With which cognitive distortion do you identify?

_____

_____

_____

Teacher Practice: Over the next week, try to pause and notice distorted thinking. You might simply note, "ah, there are the *shoulds*, again," or "this is catastrophizing," then shift your attention back to an anchor like the breath or the sounds around you.

Reacting on Autopilot

Reactions are like programs that automatically run without our conscious consent. They are often called the *low road* in the brain, because they bypass the home of foundation skills, the prefrontal cortex (PFC). These reactions begin with a stimulus, or *trigger*, that enacts the cycle. Some trigger-reaction cycles are helpful, like seeing a car careening toward you – the trigger, and jumping out of the way – the reaction. Others are unhelpful, like reading an email from a challenging parent – the trigger, and feeling angry and losing your temper with your students – the reaction. Mr. Brown and I were stuck in a cycle of reactivity. My presence triggered a pattern of negative thinking, emotion, and behavior in him, and vice versa. When he placed my name tag *under his* outside the classroom door rather than *beside his* as I requested, stress hormones coursed through my body. We spent the year agitating one another, which

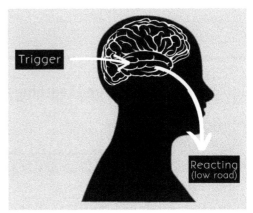

negatively affected our teaching abilities, our mental health, and our students' learning. Mr. Brown's behaviors were not the problem – the way my brain interpreted and reacted to them was.

Looking at human interactions through this lens, the other person is rarely to blame. It's actually the brain's learned interpretation of the situation, which can conjure up difficult emotions, stressful thoughts, or outward reactions. Let's say, for example, a few teachers have just been told by their principal to run yet another committee. This is the trigger. One teacher may think, "are you kidding me? I have ZERO time for this," whereas another may think "Sure, no problem." Both are reactions to the same trigger, but different brains process and react differently.

Teachers interpret the behaviors of their students, administrators, and parents based on temperament, life experience, and emotional style. However, over the years I have collected some commonly reported school experiences that enact unhelpful trigger-reaction cycles for teachers.

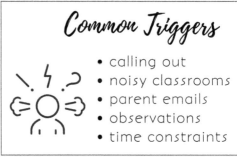

Common Triggers

- calling out
- noisy classrooms
- parent emails
- observations
- time constraints

Just as triggers differ from teacher to teacher, so do reactions. Some reactions are more overt – teachers may raise their voices, make sarcastic comments, slam doors, or storm out of rooms. Other teachers react internally – developing anxiety, headaches, body tension, or ruminating thoughts.

✎ Pause and Reflect

What are your triggers? How do you react?

_____

_____

_____

Turning Off Autopilot and Learning to Respond

Hustling through the busyness of the school day constantly triggered by students, colleagues, and unexpected situations is how many teachers end up functioning on autopilot. The day is a series of triggers and reactions, resulting in a load of stress and fatigue. As discussed in Chapter 5, allowing stress hormones to simmer in the body for prolonged periods leads to physical, emotional, and mental health decline. The first step in disabling these reactivity cycles is to shine the flashlight of attention on them with kindness, compassion, and curiosity. As the saying goes, we cannot change what we don't acknowledge. Recognizing reactivity cycles affords teachers the choice to take action and change them. With mindful awareness, teachers can create space to pause, breathe, and consciously respond to the ups and downs of the day.

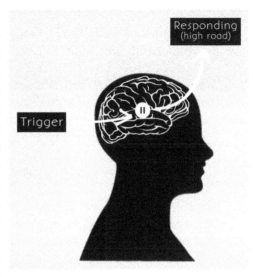

Responding is often called taking *the high road* because when teachers respond, they engage the foundational skills of the prefrontal cortex – like inhibition, behavior management, and social awareness. When teachers pause and notice the trigger, they can reappraise the situation, and possibly even engage understanding and compassion. Did Mr. Brown intend to disrespect me? Probably not. Was he poorly prepared to co-teach, and overwhelmed by the students' needs and disabilities? Most likely, yes. Knowing what overwhelm feels like as I too have felt unprepared, I can choose to relate with compassion.

Teacher Lesson

Responding vs. Reacting

Over the next week, you will practice interrupting cycles of reactivity. This is a challenging skill that takes time to develop. Try to remain curious and open to new insights, and do not beat yourself up if you do not master this right away.

> **Responding vs. Reacting**
>
> **Notice Your Trigger**. Begin to notice your patterns of distorted thinking. Pause and notice feelings of agitation, annoyance, or anger at others. Try to trace your experience back to the trigger. What set the negativity into action?

Know Your Reactivity Cycle. Once the trigger is identified, spend a few days noticing how your body and mind reacts. Do your muscles tense? How does your breathing change? What thoughts do you notice?

Choose a Response. Next, choose a response to the trigger. The response may be to simply pause and breathe, or to resist the urge to speak or act. You might choose to respond with a mental note, *ah, this is a trigger.* Another response might be to shift your attention to a stable anchor like the soles of your feet. Maybe the response is to physically move your body in some way – squeezing and releasing your hands, or walking away.

Practice. After you have chosen a response, begin to practice using it when triggered. At first you may notice that you are still reacting on autopilot, and that is okay. As soon as you catch yourself noticing the trigger or reacting, gently shift into responding. Over time, responding will become second nature!

Tips for Success

◆ As you are learning to interrupt cycles of reactivity, work with a trigger that appears often in your day-to-day, giving you ample opportunities to practice.

◆ Many teachers have been operating on autopilot for years, sometimes decades. Learning to respond rather than react to life's triggers is essentially rewiring the neurons in the brain to create new patterns of thinking and behavior. This takes time, willful effort, and self-compassion.

Pause and Reflect

After practicing for a week, come back and reflect. What new insights do you have? What did you learn about your cycles of reactivity? What was challenging? How did noticing your triggers change your interactions with others?

_____

_____

_____

Five-Minute Student Microlesson

Impulse Control

This microlesson is designed for students aged 7–12. See notes for older or younger students.

Concepts

Sometimes when we feel angry (or frustrated, offended, silly, etc.) we may react without thinking. It's as if our body automatically acts. This can get us into trouble, because we often wish we hadn't (talked back to our parents, said something mean/offensive, or behaved inappropriately).

Noticing when we impulsively react allows us to pause, breathe, and choose a different response.

Why is this important?

Choosing our responses rather than reacting impulsively almost always results in a better outcome at school and at home. Mindfulness practices help us get better at responding vs. reacting to situations that leave us feeling upset, angry, distracted, etc.

Delivery

Hook: Teacher asks a student volunteer to come to the front of the room. Toss the student a small/lightweight object, advising the student to try NOT to catch it by keeping his/her/their hands at his/her/their sides (e.g., sticky notes, paper clip, a small ball). Have the student share what it felt like to try to resist the impulse to react and catch the object.

Optional: After modeling, have students try this with partners. Point out that it feels awkward and challenging to resist the impulse to catch the object.

Demonstrate: T: "When someone throws an object to you, you have a reaction to catch it. It's not something you think about – it happens automatically. Some reactions are helpful – like catching objects or moving out of the way when someone walks too close in the hallway. Other reactions can get us into trouble, like talking back to a teacher, pushing someone on the playground, or sending a text message without thinking."

Participate: T: "Let's try responding vs. reacting. Take out a book/something to read. I'm going to create some distracting noises around the room. You might stop and notice me, then choose to respond by taking a breath and focusing your flashlight of attention on your job – reading." The teacher spends 30 seconds stomping around the room, opening and closing doors, sharpening pencils, banging on a desk, etc. Students will giggle, which is okay! T: "Okay, stop reading. Turn and talk to a partner – what was it like to *choose a response*, notice me then continue to read, rather than become completely distracted and off task?" Emphasize that it is challenging.

Thread: T: "Let's practice noticing the ways we react vs. respond to distractions during class. You also might notice how you can respond to challenging situations at home or at school."

Model: *(examples)*

T: "I feel really excited about the upcoming winter concert, and I'm noticing how hard it is to stay focused. I can't wait! I'm going to respond to this feeling of excitement by pausing and choosing to focus my flashlight of attention on my assignment."

T: "Usually when I ask you to take out your writing folders many of you moan and groan. I understand that writing can be challenging, and it's okay to feel intimidated by it. When I give this direction today, notice your reaction – what happens in your mind and body?"

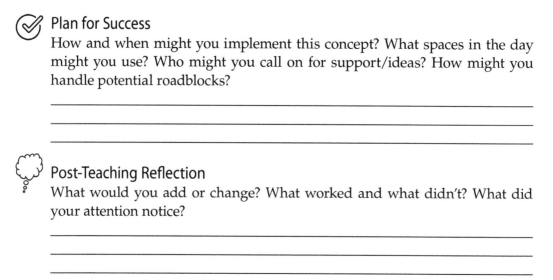

Plan for Success

How and when might you implement this concept? What spaces in the day might you use? Who might you call on for support/ideas? How might you handle potential roadblocks?

_____

_____

_____

Post-Teaching Reflection

What would you add or change? What worked and what didn't? What did your attention notice?

_____

_____

_____

Lesson Differentiation, Modification, and Notes

Trauma-Informed: Students with a history of trauma may have underdeveloped foundational skills. This is a powerful lesson for students who struggle with impulsive behaviors (e.g., keeping hands on their own bodies, calling out, poor behavior regulation, etc.) To reinforce the concept, it may be helpful to repeat the *participate* component of the lesson one to one or in small groups.

Neurodivergent: Students with disabilities often benefit from repeated exposures to this lesson. Creating explicit situations where students can practice managing impulses builds foundational skills like inhibition and behavior management. You might ask, "What do you sense in your body when you have the urge to react?"

English Learners: Preview key vocabulary: impulse, respond, react.

Gifted Learners: It is important to note that academically gifted does not necessarily equate to highly self-regulated. This lesson, among others, provides an opportunity to showcase average-performing students as "expert focusers" or "gifted impulse controllers."

Notes:

★ Consider this an introduction to impulse control for younger students (K–2), who may need continued reinforcement of the skill. Capitalize on teachable moments throughout the day, praising students for managing impulses (e.g., resisting the urge to talk in the hallway, walking instead of running to the lunchroom, etc.).

★ Rather than the teacher creating distractions, older students (middle and high) may benefit from a candid partner or small group discussion about the importance of thinking before acting, and consequences of acting impulsively.

Reference

Goeke, J. (2020). *The Co-Teacher's Guide*. Routledge.

8

The Lie

To Be a Good Teacher, I Must Work around the Clock to Make Everything Perfect

The Truth: Good teachers hold high standards while holding themselves with compassion.

 Key Concepts in This Chapter:

★ Many teachers have perfectionist tendencies, whether they realize it or not.
★ Perfectionism is underpinned by the need for control, safety, and belonging.
★ The inner critical voice is a common phenomenon that can be mitigated with mindful awareness.
★ Self-kindness, when formally practiced, can soften self-criticism and perfectionist tendencies.

How many teachers do you know that stay awake well past their bedtime to craft the perfect lesson? "I'm anal," the art teacher would say, as she moved students' desks to precisely match up with the carpet edge. Whereas an appropriate level of striving and conscientiousness may serve teachers well, many educators fall into the trap of all-or-nothing perfectionism. Interestingly, most teachers claim they are not perfectionists, either because they lack self-awareness or because they don't want to be judged. Some teachers claim they "just have high standards" for themselves and their students, while other teachers do not even realize how perfectionism is showing up in their teaching.

DOI: 10.4324/9781003316275-8

Identifying as anal retentive is socially acceptable and maybe even humorous, but being a self-proclaimed perfectionist carries a negative connotation.

When teachers become overly rigid and relentlessly hard on themselves, they hold unrealistically high standards for how things must be done. This increases stress levels without necessarily improving the quality of work. Similarly, too little attention to detail also diminishes the finished product. Teachers operating in the zone of peak performance have just the *right amount* of self-discipline and scrutiny.

It takes self-awareness, a foundational skill, and practice to put forth *just enough* diligence and attention to detail without tumbling over the edge into over scrutiny. Many teachers struggle with perfectionism, and admit that it negatively affects teaching and learning. Deeply rooted in perfectionist tendencies is the need to be in control. Most likely if a teacher is a perfectionist, the need for control is also present.

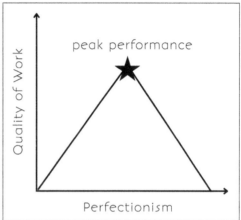

"My perfectionism makes me stress myself out and then I give up – because I'm too stressed."

Kindergarten teacher

Allowing Students to Take the Wheel

I once led an elementary school assembly which helped students build foundational skills. Classmates stood in a circle holding the edges of a tablecloth, maneuvering it carefully to keep golf balls from rolling through the slits cut into the cloth. The students practiced foundational skills like self-management, social awareness, attention, and more. Most students enjoyed the activity, while their teachers had a good laugh watching the golf balls roll across the gym. Unfortunately, one class had the opposite experience. Mrs. Hernandez clearly wanted to remain in control, and struggled to let her students problem solve without her input. She repeatedly yelled at her third graders, "No! You need to hold it up," and "Guys! Watch the ball!" At one point she even inserted herself into the game and took the lead, leaving her students stressed and anxious as they tried to comply with her demands. The purpose of the game was lost.

"Some try hard to please me. I might even give my students anxiety because I can be so picky."

6th grade teacher

📝 Pause and Reflect

How does your need for control and perfectionist tendencies show up in the classroom, if at all?

_____

_____

_____

"My perfectionism makes me too controlling. Sometimes I forget to let students just discover and explore. I will give students manipulatives with all good intentions but I've been known to go at it myself – guiding them too much because I want perfection."

2nd grade teacher

Perfect Is Good ... Right?

Perfectionism is defined as holding high standards of performance, overly critical evaluation about one's behaviors, fears and doubts of one's actions, and over-concern about other's evaluation and criticism (Frost et al., 1990; Hewitt & Flett, 1991). It is rooted in the human need for acceptance. The message from society is: in order to be accepted, be perfect.

> **The message from society is: in order to be accepted, be perfect.**

American schools, largely focused on academic goals and achievement, standardized learning targets, and evaluative grading systems *encourage* perfectionism in teachers and students. Everyone is striving for the A. I received a text from my niece reporting that she earned a 98 percent on her math final, only losing 4 out of 152 points, to which I responded "Wow! Yay!" She texted back to say that her 12-page Spanish final was her "downfall" – she earned a 93 percent. I thought, *when did 93 percent become the new failing grade?* Teachers often complain about students who *want to know exactly what to do to get the A.* They ask me how to create students who love the process of learning, rather than fixating on the final product. Parents, too, are sometimes baffled by their child's obsession with earning perfect grades, taking all AP classes, and staying up until midnight to complete assignments. Students today live within an education system that favors perfect grades over learning, *by design*. Whether parents hand out money for grades, or completely ignore report cards, it does not change the fact that our children are swimming in a system where their self-worth becomes tied to mastering an arbitrary set of grade-level content standards.

Voices from the Field

One teacher in a high-achieving suburban district shared,

> My perfectionism often has me worried a colleague or administrator will come into my room and *catch* me not being perfect. Sometimes that causes me to miss opportunities to make organic connections with my students in the moment and miss teachable moments with them.

Another said,

> When I let my perfectionism affect my teaching, I don't have the ability to be flexible and differentiate spontaneously to meet the individual needs of my students. There are unexpected things added to our agendas each day, and when I try to always follow a plan perfectly, I am constantly disappointed.

Perfectionism contributes to teacher burnout and perhaps more concerning, perfectionistic teachers may unconsciously encourage these tendencies in students by modeling these behaviors in the classroom. One high school student shared the following:

> When I can sense a teacher is a perfectionist, it makes it almost impossible to feel like I'm doing anything right. If nothing they ever do is up to their own standards, how will anything I ever submit be good enough?

Inner Critic

A teacher sits at her desk writing a lesson while playing whack-a-mole with self-disparaging thoughts. In just a few minutes her thoughts bubble up:

"This lesson is terrible."
"You will never finish this."
"Why would anyone allow you to do this job?"

Inner Critic + Perfectionism

Imagine if her principal was standing over her yelling these phrases as she tried to work. There is no way she would be able to perform, let alone perform well. Yet, this is the reality for many teachers – mentally berating themselves all day, hoping that self-deprecating comments can provide the needed motivation to work harder and faster. The **inner critic** is the voice in a teacher's head that is constantly assessing, judging, directing, and criticizing. Perfectionism makes the voice of the inner critic louder and more aggressive. Imagine handing a megaphone to a drill sergeant while trying to teach your class. Not enjoyable or productive!

Mindful Awareness and the Inner Critic

It is not necessary to examine why teachers (and most humans) have an inner critical voice, although much has been written on the topic in the field of psychology. One strategy to help quiet the inner critical voice is to name it. It sounds silly but identifying your inner critic as Negative Nancy, Beastly Brian, or Mean Megan places a healthy distance between *your awareness* and *your thoughts*. Mindfulness practices train teachers to curiously and kindly notice and label thoughts as *mental events*. Once aware of inner critical thoughts, teachers can choose whether or not to believe them and suffer under the wrath or dismiss them as simply passing thoughts that need not distract us out of the present moment. The first step is to use selective attention to *notice thinking*.

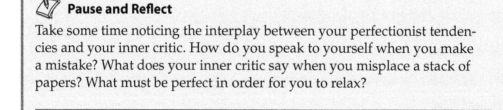

Pause and Reflect

Take some time noticing the interplay between your perfectionist tendencies and your inner critic. How do you speak to yourself when you make a mistake? What does your inner critic say when you misplace a stack of papers? What must be perfect in order for you to relax?

_____

_____

_____

As a young teacher I believed the lie that **in order to be a good teacher, I had to work around the clock to make everything perfect** – stapling and re-stapling my bulletin board until it was *just right*. I was surrounded by hustle culture – teachers stayed after school to work late and sent emails at 9:00pm. I absorbed this idea that teaching was a 24/7 commitment. I had to overextend myself, because *that's just what needed to be done*. Self-comparison feeds the inner critic. Stop and notice when you are comparing yourself to other teachers. There will always be teachers who are more creative, more organized, have better classroom rapport, or convey more confidence and ease. Holding yourself up against others is a recipe for a loud inner critic and a whole lot of suffering.

Turning toward Rather Than Away

Just as with stress and strong emotions, the way to manage the inner critical voice is to turn *toward* it rather than away from it. Becoming curious about the inner critic provides insight. For example, because I know that my inner critic is very active when I am doing anything outside my comfort zone, I am on the lookout during these times. Slowly and with practice, teachers can redirect their attention back to the present moment rather than allowing inner critical thoughts to dictate mood, mental health, and self-esteem. Here are a few strategies to manage the inner critic:

1. Befriend It: When the attention notices this voice, simply smile and accept it as one of the players in the game. Notice it, welcome it, then let it go. Do not believe it, or add to the thoughts. Adopting a kind and compassionate stance toward the inner critic decreases its power and threat.
2. Get Logical: Many claims the inner critic makes are downright wrong or unreasonable. First, dump all of the inner critic's thoughts onto paper. For each thought, ask *what evidence do I have to support this statement? Is this 100 percent true?* Logic unravels the thoughts, helping the inner critic to eventually subside or at least take a back seat. This is a great strategy for students and teachers alike.

Table 8.1 A high school student uses the Get Logical strategy to overcome her fear of driving.

Inner Critic Thought	Evidence in Favor (%)	Evidence Against
You're so stupid	0	I have good grades, am a great student, and can learn new things
There's something wrong with you	0	There is nothing inherently wrong with me. I am feeling nervous, and that is a normal and common human emotion
You are a horrible driver	0	I have driven multiple times on local roads without any mistakes

3. Talk Back: When a critical thought comes up, hit the pause button and respond. Silently say "That's not true," or counter the thought with a positive affirmation. Inner critic claiming you're a terrible teacher? Look at yourself through your students' eyes. Feel the adoration and love they have for you. Respond to your inner critic with, "I'm an awesome teacher," or "My best effort is good enough."

The inner critic is just another collection of thoughts – another object of the mind that arises and passes. Teachers do not have to believe self-critical thoughts just as they do not have to believe their cognitive distortions.

Self-Kindness

My first formal observation was a challenging experience. I was so nervous I could barely sleep the night before. Unfortunately, my lesson did not go as well as I planned. I babbled and did not execute well. The thoughts arose almost immediately after the observation ended. They went from "that experience was terrible" to "I am terrible." I allowed my judgment of a work-related mishap to affect my view of myself as a person. In 1990, Sharon Saltzberg, a world-renowned Buddhist meditation teacher, had a conversation with Gyalwa Rinpoche – the 14th Dalai Lama. She asked him, through the interpreter, "What do you think about self-hatred," to which he responded, confused, "What is that?" (https://www.sharonsalzberg .com/sit/) It appears that self-hatred is very much an American problem, spurred by constant striving for wealth, status, and power. Americans struggle with "enoughness" – feeling satisfied with what they presently have, and who they presently are.

Babies see themselves in the mirror, lean over and give their reflection a wet open-mouthed kiss. Imagine teachers kissing their reflections? Educators struggle to accept compliments, let alone express actual love for themselves. Mel Robbins, the author of *The High 5 Habit*, suggests that people give themselves a high five in the mirror every morning coupled with some self-affirming phrases. Sounds silly, but as a best-selling author and world-renowned speaker, I believe she is on to something.

Teacher Lesson

Self-Kindness

Actively practicing self-compassion gives teachers space to ease perfectionism, and accept their best effort without tumbling into over scrutiny.

Spend the next week getting to know your inner critic. Maybe give it a name to help provide a healthy distance between you – the observer, and the thoughts. Remind yourself that it is normal to have these thoughts, and that you are not alone! Next, choose a strategy: befriend, get logical, or talk back. Record your noticings here.

Inner Critic Thought	Befriend	Get Logical	Talk Back

This guided mindfulness practice will direct some gentleness and care to yourself. Use this practice when you are feeling overwhelmed or stressed. You might record yourself reading the script then listen back, or visit www.rootsandwingsonline.org for a link to a guided practice.

Time: Ten minutes

Frequency: I like to use this practice once a week when I first wake up. It has been particularly helpful during times of high stress.

Self-Kindness for Teachers

Take a moment to find a comfortable seated or lying position. Make whatever adjustments you need to be comfortable, warm, and stable. Remove your glasses, maybe your shoes, and whatever feels restrictive. Drop your shoulders down your back, soften in your hips, and let go of any tension in your jaw. Take a deep breath in through the nose and out through the nose. Notice this shift from doing to simply being. It can sometimes feel indulgent or uncomfortable to simply stop and make time for yourself. If your inner critic is barking at you with comments like, "You're too busy for this," or "You should be doing work," just simply notice that. Shift your flashlight of attention to the tip of the nostrils. Sensing the air moving in and out of the nose, feeling the rise and fall of the chest. Spend two to three minutes settling the attention on the sensations of the breath before you proceed. Next, call to mind someone who loves you. This can be any person – your child, your parent, your spouse, or even your beloved pet. Think about how this person views you. What about you is loveable? Place your hands over your heart if that feels comfortable. Breathe in and breathe out, feeling the rise and fall of the chest. Begin to connect with your inner goodness, viewing yourself through the eyes of a loved one. Let's offer ourselves phrases of kindness. It's okay if this feels forced or artificial at first. Trust the process, and repeat these phrases to yourself. Breathing in and breathing out.

May I be well.

May I be peaceful and at ease.

May I be free to live and love fully.

May I recognize my own goodness and worth.

May I forgive myself for my mistakes.

May I offer myself the same grace I would a close friend.

May I be satisfied with the *just right* amount of effort.

May I set and hold boundaries.

Repeat these phrases to yourself, noticing the sensations in your chest, throat, and abdomen. Notice any emotions that may arise. End with three to five breaths, shifting your focus back to the nostrils.

Tips for Success

♦ At first the practice may feel contrived, uncomfortable, or even greedy. Notice judgments as simply thoughts, and allow them to pass through your awareness. With practice, self-kindness can become your natural response in times of stress and challenge.

♦ It is okay to adjust the phrases to better fit your needs. You might try phrases like, "May I accept myself just as I am," or "May my best efforts be good enough."

♦ Feeling strongly averse to practices around self-kindness or self-love is an indication that it is most likely really needed!

Pause and Reflect

What did you learn about your inner critic this week? What did you notice while using the Self-Kindness Practice?

_____

_____

_____

Reflections from teachers:

'This was extremely eye-opening. I never realized how mean I am to myself! I would never speak to a friend the way I speak to myself."

"The Self-Kindness practice was tough. I had to force myself to do it. Says a lot, right?"

"For some reason I don't feel like I deserve to be kind to myself? What is up with that?"

Five-Minute Student Microlesson

This microlesson is designed for students aged 8–11. See notes for younger and older students.

Inner Bully, Inner Buddy

Concepts

Speaking to ourselves with encouragement changes the way we feel and how well we are able to complete schoolwork.

Delivery

Hook: (anecdote) Teacher tells a true story about a time when she/he/they were self-critical. Example:

> *T:* Before we begin the Spanish test, I want to share a quick story with you. I have told you before about how I'm not a great baker, right? Last night I had to bake 2 batches of cookies for my daughter's birthday. As I started the first batch, I noticed these thoughts in my head saying, "You're the worst baker!" "You dummy – why are you trying to bake?" "These will NOT taste good!" I was being so mean to myself in my mind, and it was not helping me at all. I kept getting egg shells in the batter, and measured the milk wrong twice! Thumbs up if you have ever noticed a mean voice in your head, criticizing what you're doing. Turn and talk to share when you notice this inner bully voice." Students turn and talk to share an idea.

Demonstrate: T: "There is another voice in my head called my inner buddy. She is kind, loving, and reminds me of how awesome I am. When I started the second batch of cookies, I shifted my flashlight of attention to this voice. She said, 'You got this!' 'Take your time!' 'These will be delicious!'"

Participate: T: "We are about to take a test. Let's try to focus our flashlight of attention on our inner buddy, so our inner bully will quiet down. Help me write down some phrases on the board that our inner buddy might say to encourage us to do our best work." Teacher collects phrases from students to create a list on the board. Teacher could also make a T chart, inner buddy/inner bully, time permitting.

Thread: T: "During our test, we will pause and shift our attention to our inner buddy to keep us motivated and feeling positive."

Model: *(examples)*

T: "I see some students are already finishing page 1. Let's direct our flashlight of attention to our inner buddy telling us to take our time and work carefully."

T: "It's been 15 minutes of working on this test. Let's pause and pat ourselves on the back. Listen to some kind words from your inner buddy! Who would like to share something aloud?"

Lesson, Differentiation, Modifications, and Notes

Trauma-Informed: Students with a history of verbal abuse or self-harming behaviors may openly share harsh criticism they have received from others, or say to themselves. Be prepared to address these comments with a follow up conversation or suggest discussing with a counselor. You might also preview the lesson with a student who you know to be experiencing depression or struggling with mental health challenges.

Neurodivergent: Students with learning challenges often express disparaging self-talk like, "I'm so stupid," or "I suck at math." Use this lesson as an opportunity to explicitly coach these students in replacing this language. You might even keep a post-it with inner buddy phrases on students' desks as a reminder to practice self-encouragement.

Gifted Learners: Students needing an extension might research how the inner critic voice is formed and report back.

Notes:

★ Older students (grades 6–12): You might have a more candid discussion about the "inner critic" and "self-kindness" to keep the lesson age appropriate. During the hook you may use an anecdote about self-judging inner dialogue when completing an academic project. In lieu of making an anchor chart, you might have students jot on a sticky note some positive phrases to focus on like, "I got this," "I am smart," or "stay focused on your goal."

★ When teaching students younger than eight, use discretion in discussing the inner bully. It may be more appropriate to focus solely on developing *inner buddy* speech, since younger students are still developing inner dialogue and awareness of thinking.

Tips for Success

◆ Be sure to choose a real or realistic anecdote. Students know when an anecdote is inauthentic and it detracts from the lesson.

◆ Threading foundational skill concepts into your teaching is the most important piece of the lesson. Modeling and cueing assists students in adopting and using the strategies.

◆ This lesson is meant to serve as a springboard for additional conversations about inner dialogue and self-compassion. All of the microlessons are designed to be revisited and retaught.

Plan for Success

How and when might you implement this concept? What spaces in the day might you use? Who might you call on for support/ideas? How might you handle potential roadblocks?

_____

_____

_____

Post-Teaching Reflection

What would you add or change? What worked and what didn't? What did your attention notice?

_____

_____

_____

9

The Lie

Teaching Is Easier When I Can Close My Door and Do My Own Thing

The Truth: In times of overwhelm, we need connection rather than isolation.

 Key Concepts in This Chapter:

★ Teachers self-isolate when stressed and overwhelmed.
★ Doing what is best for students is sometimes against district mandates.
★ It is easy to fall prey to *us vs. them* thinking and behaviors.
★ Human connection and relationships among staff help prevent burnout.
★ Human beings are more similar than different.

Closing the Door – How Did We Get Here?

"Just close the door and do your own thing," was the advice I was given during my first week of in-service training. My mentor, Mrs. Del Campo, had been teaching for 25 years, and swore by these words which confused me at first. "Close my door and do my own thing?" I thought, "Versus what?" She was, I found out, warning me for what was to come – a week of new teacher training during a hot and humid August week, where multiple administrators would dictate how I *should* teach the students I had yet to even meet. I was advised to nod, smile, and agree *to comply* with the district's standardized lesson plans and curriculum guides. Despite the district's rigid rules, Mrs.

DOI: 10.4324/9781003316275-9

Del Campo ultimately gave me permission to close my door and decide for myself. And at that time, I did.

Pause and Reflect

Do you agree that teaching is easiest when you can close your door and *do your own thing*? Why or why not?

_____

_____

_____

Nearly 100 percent of educators, informally surveyed, reported that closing the classroom door and being left alone was the *easiest* way to teach. When left unexamined, the belief that teaching is easier when teachers *close the door* leads to teachers fracturing off into silos. "I do not have the bandwidth to do one more thing" is a belief echoed by many educators today, and is often accompanied by a feeling of overwhelm. As detailed in Chapter 6, overwhelm occurs when the demands of the situation exceed the resources at hand.

When teachers experience overwhelm for an extended time period, closing their classroom doors and isolating serves as a coping mechanism.

This reaction mirrors the shut-down survival mode discussed in Chapter 5. Herein lies the problem and the truth: When humans experience overwhelm, they need to seek *connection*, not isolation. So why don't they? It is because a chronically stressed and overwhelmed teacher becomes easily caught in the false belief: *I should be able to handle this myself.*

Initiative Overload

I remember feeling like my head might explode as I walked out of my district's three-day literacy training. I was just getting comfortable with our current reading curriculum, yet it was already being scrapped for the next shiny new trend. Constantly changing initiatives are a major stressor educators face. Each initiative brings new materials, more training, new assessments, more time away from students, and most importantly, more stress. Many teachers have boxes of discarded curricular materials collecting dust in their classroom closets, tucked away *just in case* the district switches back. No other profession requires its employees to change what and how they work year after year. Is it any surprise that teachers are overloaded?

I am often hired by school districts to provide professional development during the few precious weeks prior to a new school year. In preparation, I ask administrators what other trainings teachers will attend while they are also trying to squeeze in time to set up their classrooms – the most important task, by far. The list of workshops never ceases to amaze me. I am told things like, "We have a new math curriculum, updated science standards, a DEI (diversity, equity, inclusion) initiative, and a new principal at the elementary school who is encouraging PBL (problem-based learning)." School board members, parent groups, and administrators all push personal agendas, often overriding the expert who is actually trained to make curricular decisions – *the classroom teacher*.

With stakeholders constantly in flux, teachers struggle to keep track of constantly changing learning targets. Many initiatives are never fully funded nor do they remain in place long enough to see real results. Can you imagine spending the time and money to train a hospital full of doctors in a new procedure just to say "sorry, nevermind, we don't have enough supplies for everyone." Laughable I know. But it's also disheartening, because teachers experience this all the time.

Closing the Door to "Do What's Needed"

"I am afraid of getting caught doing anything other than math, but they need it," said Mrs. Garcia, when we spoke about brain breaks during our coaching session. She noticed a need for her third graders to periodically decompress, so she began using two-minute brain breaks during her lessons. She conducted the brain breaks outside the hallway's line of sight because she feared being *caught* by her supervisor. Pause and consider this – today's standardized education system has created a culture of educators literally *hiding* in order to do what they know is best for students. Luckily, teachers are not helpless in the face of this situation. Harnessing foundational skills lays the groundwork for teachers to take the lead in educational reform.

Children learn at their own pace. Just as you wouldn't stand a baby on its feet and let go because *it's simply time to walk*, students cannot be forced to read, write, and learn before they are ready. Yet, the current education system expects students to demonstrate proficiency on arbitrary academic standards according to their grade level. The standardization of education, although well-meaning, has led to unrealistic expectations of even our youngest children. Certain states continue to use outdated early literacy methods, even after these practices have been proven ineffective. In response to the highly contested Oral Reading Fluency Dibels assessment, one teacher asked me, "how do I encourage Malakai to increase his reading speed when I know that it's at the expense of comprehension?" This is highly relatable for teachers administering timed fluency checks on emergent readers. Teachers must constantly reconcile the moral distress of being forced to use poor – yet mandated practices. In Chapter 4, the concept of demoralization was introduced as it relates to teacher stress and burnout. Specifically, when teachers feel demoralized, they grapple with "ongoing value conflicts with pedagogical policies, reform mandates, and school practices" (Santoro, 2018). It is clear to see why a demoralized teacher might close the classroom door and disengage.

Pause and Reflect

Which situations create moral discord for you? How do you reconcile feeling morally conflicted?

_____

_____

_____

Othering

Brene Brown said it best: "people are hard to hate close up – move in," (Brown, 2017). America was built upon the *us vs. them* culture which continues to permeate society now. The mindset persists because it benefits those in power. **Othering** groups of people who are perceived as *inferior* ensures that a small few hold the majority of social capital, power and control. Schools are microcosms of society, with *I vs. other* or *us vs. them* culture manifesting in classrooms and among staff. Teachers might subconsciously categorize students, parents, or colleagues as *other* based on race, gender, age, sexual orientation, socioeconomic status, or mental capabilities.

I	Other
Classroom Teacher	Administrator
General Education Teacher	Special Education or ECE Teacher
Veteran Teacher	Novice Teacher
Caucasian Teacher	BIPOC Teacher
Grade Level Teacher	Special Areas Teacher
Certificated Staff	Support Staff

Personally, I know what it feels like to fall into both categories. Although it is hard to admit, there have been times in my career when I believed I was superior to *others* because I held a certain title – like lead teacher. Early on in my role as a young special education teacher, I was *othered* by colleagues, and treated as if my opinions didn't matter. The most common othering that I see now is between teachers and administrators. Teachers say things like:

> Do they not understand that I have a life outside of work?
> I cannot believe they are taking away our prep period!
> I would love to see them try to do my job.

You may relate to these common sentiments teachers share about administration. Stuck in our day-to-day grind, overwhelmed with stress and fatigue, it is easy to fall into othering as a self-defense mechanism. However, shutting down, closing ourselves off, and putting walls up degrades job satisfaction and student achievement. Many have forgotten that school personnel – teachers, administrators, support staff, etc. are *more similar than different*, and all are on the same team. That new vice principal that never says hello to teachers by name or follows up on emails? He too is doing the best he can with the information he has. Negative Nancy down the hall who traps you in the parking lot to complain about her home life? She too wants peace, calm, and happiness. The superintendent in his flashy Mercedes? He, too, lays awake at night worrying about his college-aged children navigating a dangerous world. The next time you find yourself getting caught in an *us vs. them* mindset, look for the commonalities. Tap into shared humanity. Teaching from a place of *us vs. them* fans the flames of division and helps no one. Mindfulness practices help teachers notice this habit, and make a different choice.

✎ Pause and Reflect

What is your experience of *us vs. them* culture? What emotions does your attention notice as you read this chapter?

_____

_____

_____

Collective Efficacy

Teamwork makes the dream work, right? It sure does, but there is a step that must precede the work being done. Teachers must hold the *belief* that the dream is collectively achievable. Stanford psychologist, Albert Bandura, coined the phrase **collective efficacy**. He discovered that when teams of people believed they could reach a group goal, it drastically and positively affected their performance. "When educators believe in their combined ability to influence student outcomes, there are significantly higher levels of academic achievement" (Bandura, 1993). Based on his extensive research, John Hattie, a New Zealand professor, placed collective efficacy at the top of the long list of factors that influence students' academic success – above socioeconomic status and parental involvement (Hattie, 2016).

> **Simply put, when teachers believe they can *together* help students learn, grow, and thrive, they are more likely to collectively achieve that goal.**

Connection – A Teacher Superpower

Human beings are hard-wired to seek community. From an evolutionary perspective, our ancestors went from tribal dwellings to village life. Modern life is quite the opposite – humans are more digitally connected than ever before yet somehow incredibly lonely, anxious, and individualistic. When teachers resort to closing their doors, they are closing themselves off from others, when what would truly help is seeking *connection*. When working with groups of teachers I often ask them to shout out thanks to one another. Here are some of their comments:

- ◆ I want to thank Mrs. Kaplan for our early morning coffee chats. They help me more than you know!
- ◆ Thank you to the entire sixth grade team for your support while I had Covid. The outpouring of love was just what I needed.
- ◆ Shout out to the guidance department for your help with my second period class! I can't do it without you.
- ◆ I want to thank all of the teachers in the lower school. We are so lucky to have each other! You all keep me coming back every day.

Belonging is one of our essential human needs. Students thrive when they feel connected to their peers, and the same applies to teachers. In her book *Teacher Burnout Turnaround* (2020), Dr. Patricia Jennings names three adaptive superpowers that allow our species to survive and thrive: connection, communication, and cognition. Although modern education has spent a great deal of time and energy developing language (communication) and thinking (cognition), "until recently, we have ignored the most primal superpower: connection" (p. 14).

Healing Power of Relationships

We have all heard the stories about students needing just one adult to be their champion. Stories abound about students with traumatic childhoods who found support from special teachers who believed in them, making all the difference in their success. Teachers are trained to develop positive relationships with students. Great teachers make time to learn about students' lives: Do they have pets or siblings? What do they like to do for fun?

However, little emphasis is placed on relationships between teachers, or between teachers, staff, and administrators. If a single teacher can save a student from dropping out of school and becoming a statistic, imagine what a single teacher can do for another teacher about to walk out of the door.

My colleagues and I conducted a small mixed-methods[1] study on a course I created and taught, *Everyday Mindfulness for Schools*. The goal of the study was to understand teachers' lived experience of the course. One surprising finding was the emergent theme of connection and community. Taking the course, which is rich in experiential mindfulness practices, sharing sessions, and authentic communication, helped teachers feel more connected to their colleagues, and deepened their relationships.

Remoralizing by Finding Our Allies

Revisiting my supervisor's advice, I often wonder: What if instead of saying *"close the door and do your own thing"* she said *"my door is always open – come talk to me anytime!"* Looking back, it's possible that Mrs. Del Campo resorted to isolation to survive, and believed this was helpful advice to a young teacher like myself. That same year I developed a close friendship with two 4th grade teachers on the other side of the school building. They became my work besties – always there to chat after the final bell and to grab dinner on Friday nights. These two ladies sat in the front row and cheered me on when I was asked to present at a staff meeting, giving me the confidence I needed to talk to a room full of teachers who far surpassed me in age and experience. They once snuck into my classroom early one morning and revamped my less-than-Pinterest-worthy bulletin boards because they knew it was my most dreaded task. Finding allies at work who have your back, encourage, and inspire is a priceless gift, and can make all the difference.

---

1   Mackenzie, E. R., Fegley, S., Stutesman, M., & Mills, J. (2020). Present-moment awareness and the prosocial classroom: Educators' lived experience of mindfulness. *Mindfulness*, 11, 2755–2764. https://doi.org/10.1007/s12671-020-01483-7

Teacher Lesson

Cultivating Kindness

Connection to one another is vital not only to our success as educators but to overall health, wellbeing, and life satisfaction. All of us rely on one another in ways we do not always realize. This guided practice allows teachers to cultivate kindness and connection to all people. Visit www.rootsandwingsonline .org for a guided practice, or record yourself reading the following script, and play it back as a guide:

Cultivating Kindness Mindfulness Practice

Take a moment to find a comfortable seated posture. Place your hands in your lap and begin to focus your attention on your body. Begin to elongate your spine, feeling the crown of the head reaching up toward the ceiling while grounding down in your hips. Allow the chair to fully support your weight. Now, bring your attention to the sensations of your breath. Breathing in through the nose and out through the nose, calm and steady. Notice thoughts as they come, and allow them to pass. We will begin now to generate feelings of kindness and connection. See if you can stay open and curious to this practice, simply observing your thoughts, sensations, and emotions. Let's begin by cultivating some kindness for ourselves, then extend our circle of care outward. You may place your hands over your heart center if that feels comfortable. Silently offer yourself some words of kindness and care. Try these phrases, or create your own that feel genuine:

May I be well.
May I be peaceful and at ease.
May I be kind to myself in times of difficulty.
May I acknowledge my connection to those around me.
Breathing in, and breathing out. Repeating the phrases to yourself once more. Next, call
    to mind a loved one – maybe a family member, partner, spouse, child, or even a pet.
    Hold this being in your mind's eye. Sense their presence. Offering the same wishes to
    this person:
May you be well.
May you be peaceful and at ease.
May you be kind to yourself in times of difficulty.
May you acknowledge your connection to those around you.

Last, call to mind a person with whom you have a challenging relationship. Maybe this person has opposing political or ethical beliefs, or this person feels difficult to be around. This person, too, seeks peace and ease. Offer your phrases of kindness and connection to this person. Close the practice by refocusing your attention on your breath, resting in this sense of kindness and connection you have cultivated.

Tips for Success

♦ It is common for the practice to feel inauthentic at first, but with practice, it may come more naturally.
♦ Most people find that it is more challenging to express kindness toward the self than others. That's okay, and is precisely why this practice is so important.
♦ You may find that beginning the week with this practice helps set the tone for kindness and compassion for the days ahead.
♦ Remember that in any mindfulness practice, it is normal to become distracted by thoughts, sounds, the desire to move or "do" and more. Just notice those urges, and refocus your flashlight of attention.

Pause and Reflect
What did you notice while practicing?

_____

_____

_____

Five-Minute Student Microlesson

Teamwork Makes the Dream Work!
This lesson is designed for students aged 7–12. See notes for younger or older students.

Concepts
During this lesson, students will raise awareness of the many individuals who come together to produce everyday items like foods, school supplies, and materials.

Why it matters: Moving past tolerance to appreciation and acknowledgment for one another is greatly needed in school and in society. To be successful in the classroom and in life, we must learn to work together.

Delivery

Hook: Love it or Leave it: T: "Before we begin our (content area) lesson today, let's talk about one of my favorite things: snacks. Everyone please stand. I'm going to call out a snack food. If you 'love it,' I want you to hug yourself like you're hugging that snack. If you would rather 'leave it' because you don't like to eat it, I want you to pretend to crumple it up and throw it in the trash can." Teacher calls out several snack foods and allows students to show if they love it or leave it (e.g., potato chips, M&M's, chocolate chip cookies, vanilla ice cream, candy, etc.). *See Notes for variation for older students.*

T: "Now when I eat my favorite snack, popcorn, I usually throw a handful of it into my mouth while watching a show. I'm not really paying attention to the flavors very closely, and I'm not thinking about the food or where it came from. Thumbs up if you can relate to eating this way."

Demonstrate: T: "Let's imagine that I am sitting on my couch eating popcorn right now. Think about all of the people that had to take part in getting that popcorn to my bowl. For example, the person at the register that sold me the popcorn."

Participate: T: "With a partner, try to come up with at least five people who made it possible for me to eat my popcorn while watching my favorite movie." Allow students to work in pairs, then ask a few students to share out.

Here is a short list for reference:

Farmer who planted the corn, field workers who harvested the crops, tractor drivers for transporting corn, factory workers who processed the kernels into popcorn, machine operators to package the food, package designers, truck drivers who transported the product to stores, shelf-stockers, cashiers, etc.

Thread: T: "You see, there are so many human beings working together that affect your lives. When we pause and acknowledge the people behind our foods or even the paper we write on, the chairs we sit in, etc. it helps us connect and appreciate one another. As we learn today, we may pause and think about all of the helping hands behind the scenes."

Model: *(examples)*

T: "As you present your group project, please take a moment to first share who completed which part. What role did each student have? How was it helpful?"

T: "I have heard that our class needs frequent reminders to clean up the lunch tables. Let's take a moment to consider all of the people in our school community who make lunch time a success. We have to do our part as well."

 Lesson, Differentiation, Modifications, and Notes

Trauma-Informed: Be mindful of any students struggling with food insecurity.

Neurodivergent: Students with disabilities sometimes lack the ability to transform abstract or theoretical ideas from thoughts into fully formed, understandable sentences. Consider allowing them to either draw or write down their ideas to share with their partner or the class. Alternatively, guiding questions may also help, such as "Let's think about how popcorn is made. What does someone do first?"; "Let's think about how the groceries get to the shelf."

Gifted Learners: Naming the people who made it possible for a snack to get to a plate may not be stimulating enough for gifted learners. Once these students have created their list, ask them to number in chronological order.

English Learners: Visual aids might be helpful to show real pictures of the steps in the process of making, marketing, and selling the snack.

Notes:
- ★ Students younger than seven may need support and scaffolding to create their list during *participate*. The teacher may choose to conduct a group discussion rather than have students work in pairs.
- ★ Students aged 13 and older can give a thumbs up or down rather than playing "love it or leave it" during the hook.

References

Bandura, A. (1993). Perceived self-efficacy in cognitive development and functioning. *Educational Psychologist, 28*(2), 117–148. https://doi.org/10.1207/s15326985ep2802_3

Brown, B. (2017). *Braving the wilderness: the quest for true belonging and the courage to stand alone.* Random House.

Hattie, J. (2016, July). *Mindframes and maximizers.* 3rd Annual Visible Learning Conference held in Washington, DC.

Jennings, P. (2020). *Teacher burnout turnaround.* W.W. Norton & Co.

Santoro, D. (2018). *Demoralized.* Harvard Education Press.

Afterword

The Responsibility Teachers Carry

Teachers are the change agents of the classroom. They make or break a lesson, a unit, and sometimes – a student. The energy, attitudes, mental states, and emotions put forth by classroom teachers directly affect students – positively and negatively. Students absorb not only what is explicitly taught by teachers but what is implicit, therefore it is imperative for teachers to pause and ask themselves what else they are conveying. Students might take cues from the teacher regarding beliefs about their intelligence and abilities, influencing self-esteem and self-worth. Whether they realize it or not, teachers carry a great deal of responsibility in shaping not only students' academic abilities, but their beliefs about themselves as learners and members of the school community.

Many would agree that teacher knowledge and expertise is often underutilized. It is my intention to bring forth the untapped potential of K–12 educators, and harness that power for systemic change. Through this book and its related resources and trainings, teachers can lead the way for educational reform. Who else is better suited for this task?

Next Steps

Developing foundational skills is a life-long endeavor. In essence, there will never come a time when teachers feel they have mastered these skills and no longer need to practice. One way teachers can commit to supporting themselves and their students is developing a daily mindfulness practice. This need not be formal or take a lot of time, but finding a few practices from the book that work well for you and using them daily will prove beneficial for not just teachers, but all those interacting with teachers at school and at home.

For Product Safety Concerns and Information please contact our EU
representative GPSR@taylorandfrancis.com
Taylor & Francis Verlag GmbH, Kaufingerstraße 24, 80331 München, Germany

www.ingramcontent.com/pod-product-compliance
Ingram Content Group UK Ltd.
Pitfield, Milton Keynes, MK11 3LW, UK
UKHW031041080625
459435UK00013B/573